SMALL-SCALE POULTRY KEEPING

Ray Feltwell was an international poultry consultant and author of several books and leaflets on the subject. He was one of the world's leading experts on free-range poultry husbandry and was in regular contact with most of the organizations and trusts concerned with this subject.

SMALL-SCALE
POLTRY KEEPING

A Guide to Free Range
Poultry Production

Ray Feltwell

faber and faber

First published in 1980
by Faber and Faber Limited
3 Queen Square London WC1N 3AU

Printed by Mackays of Chatham plc, Chatham, Kent
Reprinted with corrections 1984 and 1987
This new updated edition published in 1992

© Ray Feltwell, 1980, 1992

A CIP record for this book is
available from the British Library

ISBN 0–571–16699–7

10 9 8

ILLUSTRATIONS

CONTENTS

ACKNOWLEDGEMENTS

The author is most grateful to the following for their co-operation and assistance:
Mr Jim Aley, The British Poultry Federation; Miss Rosalind Bicknell, The Egg Information Service; Mr Derek Crane; Dr John Feltwell; Mr George Hall, National Training Adviser, Poultry, The Agricultural Training Board; Mr Fred Hams, Past President, Rare Breeds' Society; Mr Chris Hann, Poultry Advisory Officer, Ministry of Agriculture; Mr David Hawks-worth, Dr A. William Jasper, West Coast United Egg Producers; Mr H. J. S. Jones, Plumpton Agricultural College; Mr David Martin, Malcolm Thompson Poultry International; Mr Richard Wells, The National Institute of Poultry Husbandry; and Miss Margaret Bonner and the editorial staff of *Poultry World*.

I am grateful also to Mrs Barbara Ellis for editorial help and to Mr Neil Hyslop for the line drawings.

Special thanks must go to my sister, Elsie, who so painstakingly searched the literature to produce innumerable references from which those that head the chapters were chosen, and to my wife, Edna, whose help at all stages in the production of the manuscript, and in my poultry keeping, made a major contribution to the book.

Introduction

The egg is smooth and very pale;
It has no head, it has no tail;
It has no ears that one can see;
It has no wit, no repartee.

Anon

Free-range eggs: one's thoughts immediately conjure up a picture of healthy hens, foraging in the farmyard or ranging over buttercup meadows and producing for the table lovely brown-shelled eggs with rich golden yolks.

Many people with a little land to spare—whether garden space, smallholding or school ground—would like to keep poultry. This can be either for eggs and meat, particularly bearing in mind the high cost of other meat, or for breeding unusual birds for show, a fascinating hobby, which is fast growing in popularity. Traditionally, poultry were the providers of 'pin-money' for the farmer's wife. Today poultry provide this opportunity for anyone who has a reasonable-sized garden or access to some pasture, a minimum covered scratching pen of 0·37 sq m (4 sq ft) a bird, and 0·186 sq m (2 sq ft) of house space.

The purpose of this book is to look at the many possibilities available. For young people who are sufficiently interested in the subject to make it their career, an appendix is included giving training details.

Unfortunately, there is just not enough land to go round to allow for all the eggs required to be produced on unlimited free range. Hundreds of acres of agricultural land are lost each year and the rising birth-rate throughout the world means that at the same time there are many more mouths to demand a share of available food.

Because of the shrinkage of land, the meaning of free range has gradually changed and nowadays the term is applied to eggs from hens on limited range or with limited outside runs, but with access to invigorating fresh air, sunshine and supplies of fresh green feed: all very important. Ample supplies of fresh air are essential for the general well-being of the birds and especially to reduce the risk of respiratory infections. Sunshine, as important to the fowl as to man, enables the bird to build up its own vitamin D. Finally, green-stuffs provide important vitamins and a valuable source of many minerals as well as being the major source of pigments responsible for the dark-yellow yolks usually associated with free-range eggs.

The majority of eggs sold as produced on free range are marketed by farmers, smallholders and domestic poultry keepers with limited ground, where the birds can be sheltered on days when bad weather makes life outside intolerable for them. The value of fresh air to birds outside has already been stressed, but it is important to see that they have plenty of it when they are shut up for the night or during days when they are kept in their houses because of rain, wind or snow.

Large-scale production of eggs and poultry meat under free-range or semi-intensive systems is no longer a viable proposition. It has been estimated that ninety per cent or more of the eggs produced in the United Kingdom are now laid by hens under full intensive systems. What a marketing opportunity this provides for those with imagination and initiative to supply the demand for 'free-range' eggs and poultry!

Fortunately, the *small-scale* production of eggs and the raising of the occasional batch of chickens, ducks, geese, guinea-fowl or turkeys can show a profit and also provide a tremendous amount of pleasure and interest. I should qualify that by saying that the profit may not always be a commercial one, but it should provide a margin over actual costs incurred.

The free-range system has other advantages over intensive systems. The first, and perhaps the most important, is that the cost of feeding can be significantly less than for the commercial producer, who has to rely entirely on the purchase of ready-made or 'compound' feeds. Household scraps as well as potatoes and other vegetables can be put to good use by the small keeper.

Another advantage is that free-ranging birds can find insects and different kinds of grit, which help to supply their nutritional needs.

The importance of good-quality range and the value of green feed cannot be overemphasized; green feed of poor quality has little food value and can be a hazard to health.

Now, what do you do if you want to keep poultry but your land available for birds is very limited or just does not exist? The answer is to keep birds in an airy well-ventilated building, preferably with an open-fronted scratching shed, on the deep-litter system.

Those people who can provide either type of accommodation will find reward not only in small financial profits but in food value. The main advantage of poultry meat and eggs is that they are a first-class balanced source of many essential nutrients — proteins, vitamins, minerals — required to maintain our health and well-being. In particular, chicken and turkey meat provides the essential B-group vitamins, is low in calories and readily digested.

Although meat from chickens and turkeys is a valuable food source, delicious meals can be produced from ducks and geese. These are poultry for special occasions and, admittedly, the meat contains rather more fat than chicken or turkey, but even the strictest weight-watcher can afford to relax the calorie count every now and then.

More and more people are becoming aware that good health is largely associated with a balanced diet and that it is the *total* diet that is important, rather than avoidance of certain foods because someone has suggested, often without evidence, that a certain food is bad for one's health.

The great virtue of the egg is that it is a perfect natural food that has not been refined, processed or enriched in any artificial way. Eggs provide an essential part of the diet and an egg a day will supply an appreciable proportion of the daily nutritional needs of an adult — more about this in Chapter Four. An egg a day is a very good custom, but neither eggs nor poultry meat supply the necessary dietary fibre that is required for general good health and digestion and which is today widely accepted as being of considerable importance. So, as most farmers would say, 'Start the day the egg and bacon way', and add some wholewheat bread and you have a well-balanced breakfast!

Many people are convinced that free-range eggs are nutritionally superior to eggs from hens on other systems. While it is not for me to make such a claim, I can point out that a 1978 Medical Research Council Report showed that a batch of free-range eggs had a higher content of certain B vitamins than deep-litter or battery eggs (p. 107). Leaving aside the question of nutritional value, those who enjoy home-produced eggs and poultry meat have no doubt that their flavour is superior to that of their commercial counterparts, especially where frozen poultry is concerned.

The importance of maintaining a high degree of hygiene at all stages of production is vitally important in poultry keeping. The free range offered to poultry should be of high quality. Under poor free-range conditions many consider that the poultry are likely to be more susceptible to infection from such diseases as salmonella because the birds may be more exposed to contamination than birds in cages.

Although the shell of an egg has nothing to do with its food value, a strong shell is a valuable asset when boiling eggs and there is a vast weight of circumstantial evidence that shells of free-range eggs are stronger than others.

All these matters are relevant to small-scale poultry keeping whether undertaken for pleasure or profit, for exhibition or for the table, I hope that the advice offered in this book will lead to your achieving the best possible results.

Chapter One

Making a Start

An egg is always an adventure
it may be different.
Oscar Wilde

Eggs, meat or pure breeds; Poultry for eggs; Poultry for meat; Hybrids; Modern hybrid strains; Shell colour; Selling eggs and poultry; Sample small-scale outlay; Ways of starting; Point-of-lay pullets; Broody hens; Buying day-old chicks; Yearlings; Table-meat birds.

EGGS, MEAT OR PURE BREEDS?

Before you make your decision about which poultry to keep you must truthfully answer three questions: 'Am I willing to go out in all weathers, morning and night, to feed and water the poultry, day after day throughout the year?'; 'Will my husband, or wife or children, be willing to help?'; 'Are there sufficient friends or members of the family to look after the birds when we go on holiday?'

If the answers are in the affirmative and the important decision is made to become a poultry producer, a number of other decisions have to be made. The first is to decide whether to produce eggs or poultry meat, or whether to keep pure breeds for exhibition purposes. The former should be self-financing, but the keeper of exhibition breeds, usually known as a fancier, must expect to dip into his pocket from time to time to maintain his hobby.

The number of birds to keep is also of considerable importance and the wise person will limit the number of poultry to the

accommodation and feed available and will not be persuaded to
have just a few extra birds. Overstocking is the quickest means of
running into trouble that I know.

POULTRY FOR EGGS

Egg production is the most popular reason for keeping poultry
and in most cases the choice will be brown-egg production. Because it is almost Hobson's choice, the newcomer will buy one of
the modern hybrids selected for high egg production rather than
a pure breed, which lays fewer eggs on account of intensive in-
breeding. The subject of pure breeds is dealt with in Chapter Six.

Where the poultry keeper's aim is to supply the household with
eggs, the decision about numbers is very simple. Allow two laying
birds for each member of the family and, with good management,
there should be plenty of eggs all the year. Sometimes a hen will
lay an egg a day for some weeks, but generally one can expect
only three to six eggs a week from each laying hen. Actual egg
production depends not only on the skill of the poultry keeper but
also on things outside his control such as the weather, the feed
bought and the strain of bird, but the aim should always be five
eggs a bird each week.

POULTRY FOR MEAT

The domestic poultry keeper should attempt to produce those
types of table poultry that do not fit into the large-scale producers' schedule, e.g. capons, turkeys, ducks and geese. There is
little reason in trying to compete with the mass-produced oven-
ready poultry available in large numbers in the supermarkets, but
there is a market for heavier and more mature birds which cannot
easily be supplied by the commercial concerns.

Many people prefer to buy fresh-killed birds rather than frozen
and this is another plus for the small-scale producer. Another
market which can be developed is that for ducklings and, in some

circumstances, guinea-fowl. And at Christmas and other holidays there is, of course, a demand for fresh-killed turkeys.

Raising a few birds for a specialist market is within the reach of many a poultry keeper. A batch of fifty or even a hundred day-old meat-strain chickens can provide an interesting hobby. These birds grow rapidly and can be killed from as early an age as six weeks, a few each week, either for the deep freeze or for neighbours, until the last are killed at about twelve weeks old. I know one small-scale producer who regularly raises a batch of a hundred capons for sale alive to a packing station, but such opportunities do not occur very often. Most of the modern hybrid meat strains are excellent and grow very rapidly. Although surgical caponization is no longer practised, the term is still used to describe larger birds—about 2·75–4·5 kg (6–10 lb) weight.

The meat strains of ducks, chickens and turkeys have been the subject of intensive research and development and the strains which produce the so-called broilers, table ducks and broad-breasted turkeys bear little resemblance to the pure stock from which they originated. The geneticists have developed birds that not only grow rapidly but also convert feed into meat in a very efficient manner. The table chickens fed on bought feed, killed at 6–7 weeks of age and weighing about 2 kg (about 4·4 lb) eat a total of just over 3·8 kg (about 8·4 lb) of feed. The majority of oven-ready birds found in supermarkets are killed at about that age and at that average weight, but small-scale producers can keep them for a few extra weeks and obtain really heavy birds.

I must emphasize, however, that the regular production of table poultry is usually outside the scope of the domestic poultry keeper, but it is certainly something that can be done from time to time. I have mentioned meat-strain chickens because these will be the popular choice, but it could just as well be a few turkeys. On the other hand, in those cases where there is ample range, careful consideration should be given to keeping a waddle of ducks, a gaggle of geese or a flight of guinea-fowl, if those are the right names!

HYBRIDS

Hybrids are chickens that result from the mating of two or more pure lines of poultry. The majority of chickens now used for commercial egg and poultry-meat production are now referred to as hybrids and the result of this mating of breeds or strains is a considerable improvement in performance.

These improved results—more eggs and improved rates of growth in table birds—are examples of hybrid vigour. Unfortunately, not all cross matings between pure breeds or distinct strains result in hybrid vigour. This is one of the reasons that the major breeding companies possess research farms. Extensive trials are necessary, with many different matings, to identify the superior lines. The factors influencing the economic value of chickens and the task of establishing the superiority of one particular mating over another are complex. It is for this reason that the geneticist who specializes in poultry breeding usually works with a computer. A list of the available hybrid strains is given in Table 1.

Table 1: Some leading hybrid strains

Brown shells	White shells	Meat production
Arbor Acres Brown	Babcock 300	Arbor Acres
Babcock B 380	DeKalb XL-Link	Anak 10 and 2000
DeKalb-Warren Sex-	H and N Nick Chick	Cobb 500
Sal Link	Hisex White	Hubbard
H and N Brown	Hyline White	Indian River
Nick	Lohmann White	ISA Vedette
Harco Sex Link	Shaver White	Peterson
Hisex Brown		Pilch
Hyline Brown		Ross 1,208.PM3
ISA Brown		Shaver Starbro
Lohmann Brown		
Shaver Starcross		
Brown & 579		
Tetra SL		
Yaffa		

SHELL COLOUR

In spite of the popular idea that brown-shelled eggs are of higher quality than white-shelled eggs, this is not really the case. There is no connection between the shell colour and egg quality.

The colour of the shell depends on the breed or strain of chicken. Some lay white, some lay tinted (Araucanas lay blue, for instance) and others lay brown-shelled eggs. It is often said that brown-feathered breeds of chicken lay brown eggs, but this is not true. Some pure breeds lay exceptionally dark-brown eggs, particularly Barnevelders, Marans and Welsummers.

Brown-shelled eggs are often more expensive in the shops than those with white shells. This is partly because strains and breeds producing brown eggs are usually more expensive to keep than other breeds. They usually weigh more than the light breeds and so require more food. The old law of supply and demand also applies; housewives demand brown eggs and are prepared to pay extra for them.

At one time the hybrid strains that lay brown eggs used to lay fewer eggs than those that lay white, but the situation has changed dramatically thanks to the work of the poultry geneticists. Nowadays there are available several strains of brown-shell layers that compare very favourably with the white. In the United Kingdom now nearly all specialist producers have switched to brown-egg production and ninety per cent or more of the chicks hatched are of the brown-shell layers; and this proportion is growing.

SELLING EGGS AND POULTRY

Where the object is to produce eggs and poultry for sale as well as for the home, the scale of the venture requires a careful estimation of costs. The most important thing is to ensure it is possible to sell all surplus produce at a price which will cover such costs. The enquiries to be made to answer these points can be described as a small-scale market survey. The aim should be to produce eggs or poultry meat with the qualities that cannot be matched by large-scale producers. In other words, go after the market that the specialist cannot supply.

After you have made sure there will be a market for the eggs and poultry, the next stage is to find out just what effect the proposed poultry unit will have on the home, the neighbours and personal finances, to establish whether the idea is a practical one. At the same time, enquiries should be made in case there are any local by-laws about the keeping of poultry.

The actual cost of eggs will depend on the number of eggs produced, which can vary considerably, and different levels of production should be shown in the estimated cost. The final task is to compare the cost of production with the cost of buying eggs in shops or direct from farms. This will allow a decision to be taken about the viability of the project.

Table 2 shows the estimated cost of production per egg for varying levels of egg yield and illustrates quite clearly the difference that egg production can make to the success or failure of the venture.

Once you decide to go ahead, it is a good idea to continue a business-like approach to poultry keeping and consider the records that should be kept. Accurate notes of feed consumption, eggs produced and bird mortality can be of considerable help in the assessment of performance so that any departure from normal can be spotted immediately and appropriate action taken.

Daily entries can be made on monthly record cards showing the number of birds, their date of hatch, purchases of feed, the eggs produced and any losses of birds. The cards should be kept either in the poultry houses or near at hand where the entries can be made at the time of action.

WAYS OF STARTING

Point-of-lay pullets

The Italians have a proverb that runs 'Better an egg today than a

Table 2: Sample small-scale outlay

1 Object
   To keep 10 laying birds to produce eggs for the family and a few extra
   for friends

2 Capital costs – House of $3 \times 1 \cdot 8$ m (10 ft $\times$ 6 ft) – (Fig. 1)
   91 m of 50 mm $\times$ 13 mm (300 ft of 2 in $\times \frac{1}{2}$ in) battening
   23·25 sq m (250 sq ft) of cladding sheets of corrugated iron, second-hand
   1 second-hand door
   5·5 sq m (60 sq ft) concrete slabs
   Wood for food hopper
   Water container

3 Annual costs
   10 point-of-lay pullets   £27·50
   250 kg (551 lb) of whole grain
   40 kg (88 lb) wheat offals
   40 kg (88 lb) vitamin, trace-mineral, protein
      concentrate
   200 kg (441 lb) home-grown potatoes, stale
      bread and other garden produce   £62·50
   Use of electricity for lighting and cooking   £ 4·00
   Medicines and depreciation   £ 8·00
                                                                £101·00
   Less value of hens at end of year   £ 8·00
                                                                £93·00

4 Annual production
   At 200 eggs per bird   2,000 eggs
   At 250 eggs per bird   2,500
   At 300 eggs per bird   3,000

5 Estimated cost per egg at different levels of egg production

Production per bird	Cost per egg
200 eggs	4·65p
250	3·72
300	3·10

hen tomorrow'. This makes sense and to my way of thinking is sound logic for the poultry keeper. So begin by buying some point-of-lay pullets, for this is the quickest means of starting egg production. The pullets, as female chickens are called until they first lay, may be bought when they are eighteen to twenty weeks old and, in the latter case, eggs can be expected within two to four weeks.

Rearing chicks from a day old is certainly interesting, but most people will want to produce eggs in weeks rather than waiting six months for the chicks to grow up. The pullets are best bought from someone who specializes in birds of this type. As a general rule egg production can be expected within a few weeks of buying the pullets and so one does not have to wait long for results.

Growing pullets can be bought when younger, from eight weeks and upward, but the pullet of eighteen to twenty weeks of age is the most popular and often the most convenient to buy. The supplier should be asked to give details of how the pullets have been managed during their rearing period and also asked for recommendations on future management. An important point is to find out the lighting programme to which the pullets have been subjected. It is worth knowing that pullets hatched in March and April generally begin to lay in October and will usually lay for a complete year before moulting.

Broody hens
The most interesting way to start is to buy a sitting of eggs and a broody hen. Unfortunately, it is becoming increasingly difficult to find broody hens. Most modern strains of hybrid have been selected for high egg production and for the absence of broodiness. There is little point, therefore, in visiting a commercial poultry farmer in the hope of finding or borrowing a broody hen.

The best chance of finding a suitable natural incubator is to call in one of the breeders of pure breeds of poultry—exhibition breeders—who may be able to help, or perhaps guide the new-comer to a possible source. Reading advertisements in the local newspaper is another good idea.

Buying day-old chicks

The next most interesting way to begin poultry keeping is to buy some day-old chicks and rear them until they start to lay at about twenty weeks. Day-old pullets are the best because 'as-hatched' chicks include cockerels as well. The day-olds should come from a reputable hatchery and whenever possible you should buy from a breeder whose hatchery is not far away. In this way the young chicks will not have to travel a long distance and so the risk of their becoming chilled is reduced. Try to visit the hatchery to collect the chicks. I advise this way of production in the second year, but not in the first. Rearing laying birds from a day old is by far the cheapest and certainly the most interesting way, but why, in the first instance, wait twenty weeks or so before sampling some home-produced eggs?

Most people become poultry breeders in order to produce eggs for the table, but if day-old pullets are to be bought and reared it is always a good idea to ask the hatchery to supply a few meat-type chickens at the same time. These can be reared with the pullets without extra trouble and will provide some excellent meals. Some may be prepared for the oven and put into the freezer.

YEARLINGS

Commercial poultry producers usually keep their laying hens for only one year of production and dispose of the birds at about sixteen to eighteen months of age. Such birds are referred to as yearlings. Generally, these birds will look a bit bedraggled, as well they might after having laid 250 to 300 eggs, and may also have started to moult. Once they have completed their moult, yearlings will lay much larger eggs than in their first year, but the number of eggs produced is usually about twenty per cent less.

Yearlings can usually be bought cheaply and some people always restock by buying such birds. The practice of buying yearlings is not one I would recommend until after some experience has been gained in day-to-day poultry management.

TABLE-MEAT BIRDS

The way to start table-poultry production is to buy day-old
chicks. This advice applies to meat-type chickens, table ducks,
geese and also turkeys, although in the last case it may sometimes
be more convenient to start with turkeys that are eight weeks old
and therefore well over the rearing period.

Guinea-fowl make ideal table birds and the day-old chicks are
known as keets. An alternative is to buy a trio of one male and
two females and build up by natural methods. More details are
given in Chapter Five.

Incidentally, the trend to the free-range system is well advanced
in France. In the La Bresse region for example the farmers have
developed a strong market for table chickens of from 1·4 to 2·2 kg.

The birds are reared in comparatively small batches on free
range and are not marketed until sixteen weeks of age. The feed
consists mainly of ground maize, milk products and the nutrients
obtained from the range. Antibiotics and coddiciostats are for-
bidden.

The birds are of very high quality and as a result have been
granted an *Appellation d'Origine*, which means that only those
birds that reach the quality standards required and are reared
and managed on approved lines can be described as being La
Bresse.

Chapter Two

Housing

Put all thine eggs in one basket —
and watch the basket.

Mark Twain

Size of house; Design; Roofs; Walls; Pop-holes; Housing for intensive systems; Housing bantams; Pole houses; Straw-sided houses; Straw-yards; Deep-litter housing; Range shelters; Fold units; Nest-boxes; Nest-boxes for broody hens; Roosting; Perches; Droppings boards; Droppings pits; Ladder perches; Fencing; Catching crate; Catching hook; Carrying crates; Plucking box.

One of the main objectives is to provide a comfortable, draught-free well-ventilated and fox-proof place in which birds can live when they have to remain indoors. Overcrowding must be avoided for this can soon lead to colds and sneezes and poor egg production. It is essential that the house has a dry floor, for dry feet and good results go together. It must also be stout enough so that even the most persistent fox cannot break in.

SIZE OF HOUSE

The first thing to decide is the size of the house and with a small number of birds it is best to be generous and allow them plenty of floor space. A good standard, where birds have access to range, is to allow 0·186 sq m of floor space (2 sq ft) a bird. Bantams require far less space than larger fowls and three bantams may be housed in the space normally given to two large birds (p. 151).

Whatever house is built it should comply with the current Codes of Welfare of the Ministry of Agriculture. The Codes act as guidelines to poultry keepers to safeguard their stock, and free copies may be obtained from the Ministry. They emphasize the importance of good management, identify those precautions necessary for the welfare of the birds, and contain advice on housing, ventilation, temperature, lighting, stocking densities and day-to-day management. Specific recommendations are made for birds kept on free range.

The poultry unit should be in a position where neighbours will not be annoyed. Normally, laying birds make little noise except when announcing the arrival of a newly laid egg. On the other hand the cockerels, with their early morning calls, cause some town dwellers to become irate. Geese and guinea-fowl can also contribute to the dawn chorus in a manner that is not the delight of everyone and so these should be confined to the country rather than the town poultry keeper.

The site should be dry; in areas where the land tends to be wet, it is a good idea to build up the base on which the house is to stand. Old bricks, stones and cinders may be used and the level raised 15–30 cm (6–12 in). Other points to consider are the supplies of water and electricity: the nearer the poultry house is to these services the lower will be the installation costs. Electricity is not an essential, but is a great help in maintaining winter egg production. As the days draw in, egg production usually falls, but by using lights the egg yield may be increased. Breeders usually advise on the best method of lighting for their strains.

In many cases the most convenient place for the poultry house is against or near a boundary fence. It is generally best to have a free-standing house 45–60 cm (18–24 in) away from the actual fence, thus leaving yourself sufficient room to get all round the house for regular maintenance. An excellent site is against an existing wall, so saving the cost of the rear wall. Wherever possible the house should face south, so that maximum use can be made of the health-giving rays of the sun, and should always be sited so that the prevailing wind cannot blow directly into the building.

DESIGN

Although a poultry house is not difficult to build, it is a good idea to prepare a design and plans before beginning. The plans need not be very elaborate but should include the position of the doors, windows and equipment inside the house. The next stage is to prepare a list of materials so these can be found in the most economic way. A visit to a demolition scrapyard is usually well worth while and can save a lot of money, but try not to give the house a 'shanty town' appearance when using second-hand materials. Nothing looks worse or annoys neighbours more than a shack.

To build a simple house for ten to twenty-five layers (Tab. 2) you need not spend a great deal of money if you make use of second-hand materials. A lean-to house with a floor area of 3 × 1·8 m (10 × 6 ft), a front height of 1·8 m (6 ft) and back of 1·37 m (4 ft 6 in), will give the birds plenty of room (Fig. 1) and will allow sufficient height for you to enter and clean the house comfortably. In addition to felt or corrugated iron for the roof, and tongued-and-grooved board of second-hand boards for the walls, you will need 5 × 4 cm (2 × 1½ in) framing timber, 5 × 5 cm (2 × 2 in) timber for perches, wire netting, hinges, chains for the shutters, bolts, and concrete slabs for the floor.

The actual design of the poultry house will depend on individual circumstances. Where ample range is available, a house that can be easily moved is the answer; it can be mounted on wooden skids or wheels if a tractor or Land Rover is available to move the house to a fresh patch of grass from time to time. Where mechanical moving aids are not available then the house should be small enough to allow it to be moved by one, or at the most two, people. In this case the house, usually called an ark, should measure 2 × 0·75 × 0·9 m (6 ft 6 in × 2 ft 6 in × 3 ft) high at the ridge and have two handles at each end. Generally a house of this

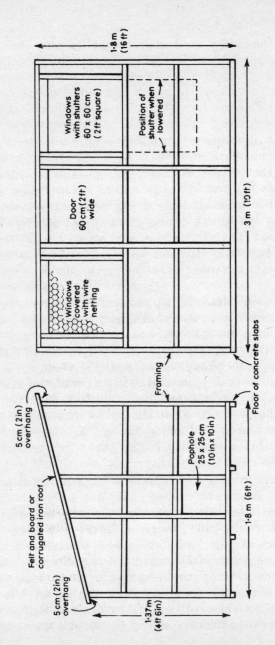

Fig. 1. Side and front views of basic lean-to poultry house for ten birds, in which use can be made of second-hand materials

Windows with shutters 60 × 60 cm (2ft square)

Position of shutter when lowered

Door 60 cm (2ft) wide

Windows covered with wire netting

1·8 m (6ft)

3 m (9ft)

Framing

Floor of concrete slabs

5 cm (2in) overhang

Felt and board or corrugated iron roof

5 cm (2in) overhang

Pophole 25 × 25 cm (10in × 10in)

1·37 m (4ft 6in)

1·8 m (6ft)

type has a floor made of wooden slats or welded wire. The slats should be made of 2.5×2.5 cm (1×1 in) battens, planed and tapered to the underside, 2.5 cm (1 in) apart. A nest-box, with access from the outside, can be placed at one end. Such a house is suitable for half a dozen laying birds. To allow sufficient ventilation at night, windows or shutters can be provided on the sides of the house with an outlet near the highest part.

Often space is limited and the birds have to be kept indoors on the intensive (also known as deep-litter) system of housing, or allowed outside to a restricted area — the semi-intensive system. One example of the latter is the straw-yard (p. 40) in which case a more permanent building may be designed with a solid floor. The cheapest house of this type is the pole house (p. 37). The more conventional house is prefabricated so it is possible to take the house down if the poultry keeper moves to another district. Framework may be made of 5×4 cm ($2 \times 1\frac{1}{2}$ in) timber, which will usually be ample for small buildings. The house sections are best bolted together and remember to use square-headed bolts. The bolts should be rubbed with Vaseline before fixing to enable them to be undone easily if the house has to be moved. The use of square-headed bolts instead of the more common round or mushroom-headed ones is to enable a spanner to be used at each end of the nut and bolt. Anyone who has tried to undo round-headed bolts after the building has been in use for some time will understand the problems these create.

ROOFS

The design of the roof is generally a matter of individual preference and an effort should be made to fit the building in with its surroundings.

A simple roof to build is the lean-to and generally it is all that is required for most small poultry houses. The lean-to roof is ideal when it is possible to make use of an existing wall to form the back of the house. Houses of up to 3 m (10 ft) wide are satisfactory on the lean-to principle. The two-third span or double-span roof is preferable for larger or portable houses. The two-third span house is convenient for a house 2·5 m (8 ft) wide and such buildings can look very attractive (Fig. 2).

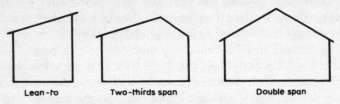

Lean-to   Two-thirds span   Double span

Fig. 2. Types of roof suitable for poultry houses

In areas where snow is likely to fall it is important to make the roof sufficiently strong to support the snow and at a sufficient angle for as much snow as possible to run off the roof.

The timbers that support the roof are of two types: the rafters are the members that run up and down, while those that run across are known as purlins. Purlins are particularly important when corrugated iron or aluminium is used for the roof, for these covering materials are fixed by nailing directly into the purlins. Rafters made of 5 × 5 cm (2 × 2 in) deal, 1–2 m (3 ft 3 in–6 ft 6 in) apart and purlins of the same size or 5 × 4 cm (2 × 1½ in) every 1 m (3 ft 3 in) are satisfactory for houses up to 2 m (6 ft 6 in) wide. Houses up to 3 m (10 ft) wide require stronger roof timbers and rafters of 10 × 5 cm (4 × 2 in) every 2·5–3 m (8–10 ft) are necessary, with purlins of 10 × 5 cm (4 × 2 in) every 1·25 m (4 ft).

The roof should extend well over the sides of the building so that any rain that falls on the roof drops away from the house. Rain-water gutters can be fitted, but are unnecessary except in cases where water has to be collected for use or removed because of drainage problems.

The roof of the poultry house is often well exposed to view and so may need extra attention. The most durable roof is one made from corrugated aluminium or iron, but these can be rather expensive unless a good second-hand supply is available. The sheets are made in lengths of 2·5 and 3 m (8 and 10 ft), the former being suitable to cover a lean-to roof of a house 2 m (6 ft 6 in) wide, and the latter for a house 2·5 m (8 ft) wide. So adjust the size of the house to the materials available. Special nails and washers should be bought and the nails should be driven into the top of the corrugations, otherwise the roof will leak. Wood covered with roofing felt can be used for the roof and looks particularly attractive if the specially-designed felt roof tiles are used.

The cheapest roof is one made with felt held in position by wire netting. Properly laid, these roofs will last for a few years. They must be well battened down or else they may be lost in strong winds. Make a sandwich with felt in the middle and a layer of 5 cm (2 in) mesh wire netting on either side. The first layer of netting is fixed to the roof and drawn as tight as possible. Then the felt, or other plastic material, is laid on the netting, making sure that all the joints are well overlapped. The roof is completed by stretching the second layer of netting over the top and drawing it as tight as possible before nailing the final battens into position.

WALLS

The framing timbers for the walls of the small poultry house can generally be made of 5 × 4 cm (2 × 1½ in) planed deal. Uprights and cross members should be about 50 cm (20 in) apart. It is important to make the framing absolutely square or it may be difficult to fit in the windows and doors. Badly fitting windows mean draughts, which lead to reduced output from the birds.

Covering material used for the walls is known as cladding and the most satisfactory for the small house is tongued-and-grooved boarding. Weather boarding may be used, but unless this is lined the house will be rather draughty and upset the birds. Exterior-grade plywood is also frequently used.

The inside walls may be lined to a depth of 30–45 cm (12–18 in) from floor level with some strong material such as galvanized sheeting to protect the sides from the effects of litter and to help keep out rodents.

Where possible, the upper half of the front of the house should

be covered with bird-proof netting so that the front can be completely open when the weather allows. To prevent wind and rain
from driving directly into the house, the windows may be hinged
at the top and arranged to open outward. An alternative is to
extend the roof of the span-roofed house to provide protection.
Another method is to make a special hood, which should be
fitted so that it does not reduce light inside.

However strong the windows appear to be, it is always a good
idea to cover them with wire netting to prevent predators from
entering the house and to keep the birds in. My wife and I proved
this the hard way some years ago when we were rearing a dozen
white turkeys. The birds were in a small studio, above a garage,
which had large windows on either side. The turkeys were no
trouble at all for the first sixteen weeks and then we had the night
of the full moon. It must have been moonlight madness for, at
about midnight, we heard a lot of noise and the sound of breaking
glass. We rushed out of the house to find that all the turkeys were
on the lawn. All we could assume was that the full moon, which at
first had been hidden by clouds, had shone directly through the
windows on one side of the house and out the other. The turkeys,
perhaps thinking that dawn had arrived, had taken off from their
perches and flown directly through the windows. We collected the
errant turkeys and returned them to their house, not one of them
apparently any the worse for the moonlight flight. We then decided, rather like locking the stable door after the horse has
bolted, that we had better buy some wire netting and cover the
windows.

Houses should be of sufficient height to enable the keeper to
work in them comfortably or, in the case of very small houses,
designed so that the keeper can reach any part of the house from
the door or lid without having to stand on his head to do so. A
convenient height at the back of a lean-to poultry house is 1·70 m
(5 ft 6 in) rising to about 2 m (6 ft 6 in) at the front, for a house of
about 2 m (6 ft 6 in) wide.

The door, opening outward, is usually best at the front of a
lean-to house and at the highest point in the side of a span-
roofed building. A very convenient arrangement is to make the

entrance door to the house in two parts, rather like a pair of stable doors. You can open the upper part of the door and lean on the lower while looking at the stock. In the summer the upper half can be left open provided a wire netting partition is installed.

POP-HOLES

The entrance by which the birds leave and enter the house is usually called a pop-hole and this should be placed in a convenient place so that the daily job of opening and closing it does not take too long. Pop-holes should be made secure and fox proof. The pop-hole needs to be about 25×25 cm (10×10 in) and not more, otherwise it might be big enough for small children to climb through in search of mischief or eggs (Fig. 1).

A wooden slide that runs up and down, is the best type of pop-hole. The slide should preferably be inside the house and the fastening, when open, should be secure, otherwise there is a danger that the birds will be accidently locked out on the very night when the fox appears on an early stroll. Similarly the shutter should be firmly secured at night so that the wily fox does not push open the slide to get at the birds.

I remember going to let out the birds one morning and was surprised that not a sound was coming from the range house. On looking inside I found that all the birds were huddled on one side of the house and a very frightened badger was huddled on the other. Fortunately not a single bird was harmed and I was able to release the inquisitive badger.

The disadvantages of pop-holes that open and close by sliding from side to side is that they can quite easily be opened or closed by accident. Sheep, a dog or a fox will often rub themselves on the outside of a poultry house, sometimes letting the birds out or shutting them out in other cases.

Once the house is complete and before the birds are housed, all the wooden parts should be given a coat of creosote or other wood preservative. The useful life of the timber will be greatly extended by this treatment. Additionally, painting with a pre-servative will help to keep insect pests at bay.

The most satisfactory house for poultry is one with a solid floor on which litter can be strewn to allow the birds to scratch. The scratching is specially valuable when the birds have to be kept in the house during periods of very bad weather. Another advantage of the solid-floored house is that the building can be used by birds of all ages, from a day old and upward, and by most species of domestic poultry.

HOUSING FOR INTENSIVE SYSTEMS

Now let us consider the needs of a flock of six laying hens or thirty-six table birds to be kept entirely indoors. A suitable house may be 2 m (6 ft 6 in) wide and 2 m (6 ft 6 in) long. A wire partition can be put across the house to allow for two groups of six bantams instead of laying hens. The house is also suitable for meat production and can be used to rear a batch of thirty-six table chickens for killing at eight to ten weeks, or for twenty birds up to sixteen weeks.

Alternatively the house can be used by eighteen to twenty layers kept on the semi-intensive system. A house of this size is very versatile and can, for example, be used for a gaggle of up to a dozen geese that spend their time on range but have to be shut up at night as protection from foxes and other predators (Pl. 9).

Although the house can be used exclusively by the birds, it is a good idea to extend the length of the building by 1 m or so (about 3 ft) to provide a small store. This is a useful arrangement which also makes it easy to fit nest-boxes in the partition wall so that eggs can be collected without actually going into the pen. Where this is done, remember to shut the outside door before collecting the eggs, for otherwise one can be certain that at one time or another one of the birds will pop out of the nest-box and fly straight out of the door.

HOUSING BANTAMS

The general principles of housing apply equally to the housing of
bantams, but of course bantams require far less room. The houses
can be made very small and designed so that all the corners of the
house can be reached from the outside without your having to go
into the building.

A suitable house for six bantams is 1 m (3 ft 3 in) wide, 1·25 m
(4 ft) long, 0·6 m (2 ft) high to the eaves and 0·75 m (2 ft 6 in) to
the ridge. The house can be mounted on long legs so that the run
can be provided underneath. Although this may be somewhat
difficult to clean, it can provide a useful scratching area if space
is limited. A run may be attached to the house and this need not
be too large, 3 × 1 m (10 ft × 3 ft 3 in) and 1·5 m (5 ft) high for
instance. The run should be boarded to a height of 45 cm (18 in)
from the ground with wire netting above.

Housing suitable for ducks, geese, turkeys and guinea-fowl is
dealt with in Chapter Five.

POLE HOUSES

Pole houses are fixed, easy to build, low-cost buildings that may
be made to a simple design using 8–10 cm (3–4 in) oak, chestnut
or larch poles. The name pole building is used because the poles
form the main structure of the house and they are cut straight
from the wood and are not expensively-seasoned imported timber.
The poles should be stripped of their bark before use. It is wise
to use gloves while handling larch poles or you will finish with a
handful of minute splinters.

The basic idea is that the poles take the weight of the roof and
the walls are merely hung on to the sides. Another feature is that
the poles are let into the ground to a depth of about 60 cm (2 ft)
after first having been treated with creosote. The poles may be
concreted into the ground or fixed by means of digging a hole,

placing the pole upright, and filling the hole gradually, tamping the soil hard. Special foundations are not necessary.

A simple pole house is one with a lean-to roof and built-in spans of 2–3 m (6 ft 6 in–10 ft). A convenient size is 2 m (6 ft 6 in) wide and 2·5 m (8 ft) long. For a larger house, add a further section. The corner poles must be square with each other. Once the uprights are fixed, the cross members on which the roof is laid are fitted. If the roof is to be of corrugated iron or aluminium, it will finish askew unless the corner poles are square. It is not so important to have the building completely square if the roof is made of roofing felt or other suitable plastic material. A felt roof, if properly fitted, will last for several years. The cross members on which the roof is laid can be poles of 5–10 cm (2–4 in) 60 cm–1 m (2–3 ft) apart (Fig. 3).

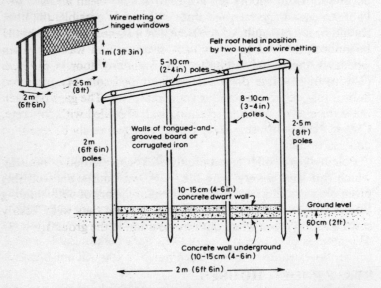

Fig. 3. An economical pole house, which can be made from inexpensive materials

The next thing to do is build a miniature retaining wall all round the house. The wall is not to take any weight but merely to help to keep out predators. The wall can be let into the ground to a depth of 10–15 cm (4–6 in) and can be built to a similar distance above to form the level for the floor. It is a simple matter to make the wall; boards are used as shuttering on either side of the poles at ground level. The space between the boards is filled with concrete to form the retaining wall. The shuttering is removed after twenty-four hours.

Any type of covering material can be used for the walls: tongued-and-grooved weather boarding, corrugated iron or even felt may be used. The front of the house may be boarded up to a height of 1 m (3 ft 3 in) with wire netting above or windows hinged at the top may be fitted to provide extra protection from the weather.

The floor can be made up of well-consolidated soil mixed with cinders, but such floors are not easy to keep clean and are also liable to encourage rats and mice. Whenever possible, the floor should be solidly built, of concrete, for instance, and this should be smooth finished to allow easy cleaning and washing down whenever the house is empty. The standard floor is 5–10 cm (2–4 in) of concrete on top of well-tamped soil. My preferred floor is made up from standard concrete slabs. The gaps between the slabs and the outside retaining wall are filled with concrete. One advantage of using slabs is that they can easily be removed and used again.

Pole buildings offer a comparatively cheap method of housing which can have a very long life. My own houses built on this principle are still in use after over twenty years of withstanding Sussex clay. Admittedly I used oak posts, but they were freshly sawn and still green when put into position in the ground.

STRAW-SIDED HOUSES

Cheap but somewhat temporary, housing can be made using straw for the sides. The framework of the house can be made in the usual way with the cladding made from a mat of straw packed between two layers of wire netting. Hay may be used instead of

straw, if necessary. The straw or hay need not be packed too
tightly and the roof of the house can also be made of straw, but is
not likely to be very satisfactory unless some advice on thatching
is taken first. Generally it is better to use an orthodox roof with
the walls of straw.

STRAW-YARDS

The term straw-yards is applied to the semi-intensive method of
housing where birds have access to a covered building and to a
straw-covered outside run or yard. The birds should be allowed
0·28–0·37 sq m (3–4 sq ft) a bird inside the building and a minimum of the same area outside. The straw-yard system is usually
unsuitable for the small-scale poultry keeper unless an ample
supply of good quality straw is available. Fresh straw is placed on
top of the old, whenever required, and the yard is given a complete
clean-up once a year. Good management is necessary, otherwise
the straw-yard becomes a wet, smelly mess and rodents are
attracted.

DEEP-LITTER HOUSING

Deep litter is the system for anyone who wants to keep poultry but
whose land for ranging is very limited or just does not exist. The
birds should be given plenty of room in an airy, well-ventilated
building, preferably with an open-fronted scratching area. An
open front allows plenty of fresh air, which helps to maintain
healthy birds, but make sure that the birds can roost in a draught-
free part of the building.

The system gained its name from the fact that the floor litter,
with good management, may be left in the house throughout the
life of the birds. Of course, some can be taken out if needed for the
garden. Similarly, if any part of the litter becomes wet this should
be removed and replaced. At the end of the laying period, the
house is completely cleaned out and the resultant litter, which

may have built up to 30 cm (12 in) or more, can be transformed into valuable compost.

RANGE SHELTERS

Range shelters are very lightweight, portable houses with a roof overhanging the sides and which are themselves covered with wire netting. They may be used for all types of growing birds kept

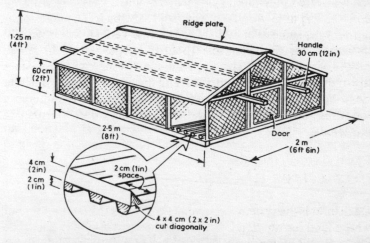

Fig. 4. Range shelter with removable slatted floor, to house forty pullets to point of lay. It is mounted on two 10 × 5 cm (4 × 2 in) skids and the handles extend through the house to act as perches. The ridge plate, to keep out the weather, is of the same material as the house

on range. Perches should be used for chickens and positioned so that the birds perch in the shade of the roof. A popular size is 2 × 2·5 m (6 ft 6 in × 8 ft). Good quality wire netting or welded wire should be used for the sides and this should be securely fixed as a precaution against foxes (Fig. 4).

FOLD UNITS

Fold units are small houses that are combined with a run in which birds are confined; they are moved to a fresh patch of grass daily. These houses are excellent for use on light and sandy soils but are not very good on heavy clay soils. The main disadvantage of fold units is the effort required to move the houses, and for this reason the units should be small and light. The units are very useful for running a breeding pen made up of one cockerel and two or three females. A particular advantage of fold units is that the birds are under control and relatively safe from foxes.

The birds in the fold unit should be allowed plenty of room and the minimum space should be 0·37 sq m (4 sq ft) per bird. Thus, a suitable fold unit for six laying birds should measure 1×3 m (3 ft 3 in $\times$ 10 ft), a fold for ten birds $1 \cdot 25 \times 3$ m (4×10 ft) and a fold for twenty-five birds $1 \cdot 5 \times 6$ m (5×20 ft).

Fold units are usually simply made so that the end section forms a triangle. They can also be made with sides of about 40 cm (16 in) with the house portion of the fold at one end and rising to 60 cm (24 in) at the ridge.

NEST-BOXES

Nest-boxes need not be expensive. Each nest should be about 30 $\times$ 30 cm (about 1 sq ft) in floor area and there should be one nest for every three to four birds. Communal nests may be used, but these are not so satisfactory as individual nest-boxes; I prefer the latter and feel that they result in fewer cracked eggs. The nest should be about 60 cm (2 ft) off the ground with a rail of 5×5 cm (2×2 in) about 10 cm (4 in) in the front of the nest. The laying bird jumps on to the rail before entering the nest. The rail may be hinged so that it can be used to close the nest at night or whenever it is not required (Fig. 5).

One of the most important aids to clean egg production is

nests in good condition, which also helps to reduce the numbers of cracked eggs. The entrance to the nest should be 8–10 cm (3–4 in) above the base of the nest to help prevent litter from falling out.

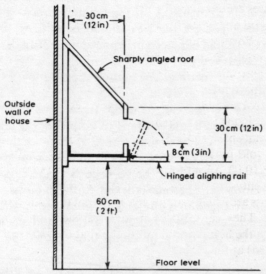

Fig. 5. Nest-box with sharply-sloped roof to prevent birds from perching on it, and hinged alighting rail

The floor of the nests can be made of wood or of 2·5 cm (1 in) mesh wire netting; my choice is wire netting because this assists clean egg production. Make sure that the birds cannot perch on top of the nests, or droppings will build up on them. Wire netting may be used to keep the birds off, or the nests can be made with an acutely-sloping roof on which the birds cannot perch.

The nests should be as far away from the entrance of the house as possible to allow the birds to clean their feet in the litter before entering the boxes, particularly important when outside conditions are muddy.

NEST-BOXES FOR BROODY HENS

A specially designed box for the broody hen is by no means necessary. I like to use a tea chest so that the sitting hen is more or less free from draughts. A strong cardboard box can also be used. Whatever is used, the box should be at least 40×40 cm (16×16 in). It should be placed in a quiet corner of an outbuilding or even in a sheltered part of the garden, if the box can be made fox-proof with wire netting. The netting should allow a small run for the hen to use for exercise.

The base of the nest can be made from grass turf of about 10 cm (4 in) deep in a saucer shape to keep the eggs in, or from sand. The base should be slightly moist. Remember the object is to prevent the eggs from rolling away from the hen and becoming chilled. The nest should not be so deep that the eggs can roll against each other and become cracked. Straw or hay is placed on the soil and arranged in a circle. This litter, clean wheat straw for preference, can be twisted into a rope and made into a circle to fit the box; dirty or damp litter should be replaced immediately.

The final preparation of the nest is to arrange a shutter so that the hen can sit in subdued light. A wooden shutter can be made, but an old sack can be used. The hen needs some ventilation, so do not enclose the box completely, particularly if a tea chest is used. If necessary, a number of ventilation holes can be drilled in the chest along the top of the sides.

ROOSTING

Poultry, except ducks and geese, prefer to roost at night provided they are encouraged to roost from an early age. Once on the perches for the night, the birds are generally out of harm and are not likely to be frightened into crowding into the corner of the house, where some of them may be trampled to death. Once the chickens are off heat, and this may be at four to five weeks during warm weather, perches may be introduced into the pen about 15 cm (6 in) above floor level.

Perches

Perches must never be a fixture in the house and should always be easily removable. In the event of an attack of red mite the perches can then be burnt and replaced with new ones.

Very satisfactory perches are made from 5×5 cm $(2 \times 2$ in) planed deal not more than 1 m (3 ft 3 in) long. The longer perches should be provided with a central support, or stronger timber used. In all cases the edges of the perches should be rounded off to make them more comfortable for the birds. Fresh-cut poles make excellent perches, but remember to remove the bark first.

Where more than one perch is to be used, those at the rear should be on a slightly higher level than those at the front. If not, the birds tend to crowd on to the first perch without leaving room for the rest.

Three types of perch should be considered and these are: perches placed over a droppings board, perches placed over a droppings pit, and perches arranged against a wall in the form of a ladder (Fig. 6).

Droppings boards

Where space is very limited this system is preferable. The perches are placed about 15 cm (6 in) above the droppings board, which is itself about 40–60 cm (16–24 in) above floor level; the lower level is used for bantams and the higher level for larger breeds of poultry. The system allows the birds more room for scratching because they have access to the area underneath the droppings board.

The perches should be at least 25 cm (10 in) from the front of the droppings board and from the back of the house, to prevent droppings from falling on to the floor at the front or piling up near the back.

Generally the most convenient place for the perches is at the rear of the house with the perches running the length of the building. Two rows of perches about 30 cm (12 in) apart will usually be sufficient; thus the droppings board need not be more than 75 cm (2 ft 6 in) wide, which is a suitable width for cleaning.

The following are the minimum allowances of perch space per bird: bantams, 10–15 cm (4–6 in); light breeds 15 cm (6 in); heavy breeds, 25 cm (10 in); turkeys, 30 cm (12 in).

Droppings boards are usually made from tongued-and-grooved boarding placed to run from the front to the rear of the house, which is the way the boards are to be scraped. Exterior grade plyboard may also be used. The droppings board should be sprinkled with sawdust or sand before use and again whenever the boards are cleaned, because this makes the task of cleaning much easier. The droppings should be removed every day for at least six days a week. To make cleaning easier, a refinement is to make perches as a frame and to hinge the frame at the rear of the house.

Droppings pits
Droppings pits are the most labour-saving method of management. The pits are really a platform about 50–60 cm (20–24 in) off floor level with perches above. Tough wire netting or welded wire prevents the birds from getting into the pit and the droppings remain there until wanted for the garden or until the birds are removed at the end of their laying year.

A popular position for the droppings pit is against the rear wall of the house. The sides of the pit should be made of a material that is not damaged by the droppings. Flat galvanized sheeting is often used. The sides of the pit should not be completely covered or troubles from smells may arise. There should be a gap of about 5 cm (2 in) immediately below the perches for ventilation. At the start, before the birds are put in the house, the bottom of the pit should be covered with a good layer of straw or old hay or peat moss. This will absorb the moisture from the droppings so that by the end of the season there will be a good supply of dry manure for the garden.

Ladder perches
The simplest form of perch is that which merely rests against the

side of the house. Three or four perches may be fixed on a frame and the frame placed against the wall of the house, at not too steep an angle. The first perch may be 30–40 cm (12–16 in) off floor level with the others at different levels. The highest perch should be at the rear and the lowest 25 cm (10 in) from the wall. Perches of this type work very well indeed if the birds are given plenty of floor space. The system is not advisable where the stocking density of a house is high (Fig. 6).

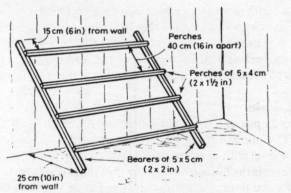

Fig. 6. Lean-to ladder perches

FENCING

Much as one may prefer to have poultry on unrestricted free range, this is not always possible because of the danger of losses from foxes and other predators. Some fencing will generally be required so that the birds can be confined to a fox-proof compound at night or when the owner wishes to go out for the day. Wire netting 2 m (6 ft 6 in) high or galvanized welded-mesh wire is the most satisfactory material to use for fencing.

Considerable care is necessary to make a wire-netting fence relatively fox proof. A small trench should be dug to a depth of at least 15 cm (6 in) and the netting then follows the course of the fence to a minimum depth of 15 cm (6 in). The netting is then laid on the bottom of the trench for 15 cm (6 in) outward from the fence, and the trench refilled to prevent foxes from digging under the wire. Unfortunately, foxes are good climbers and will not be put off by a wire fence that is only 2 m (6 ft 6 in) high. An extra 60 cm (2 ft) of netting needs to be added to the main fence and arranged at an angle, sloping upward and outward from the fence (Fig. 7).

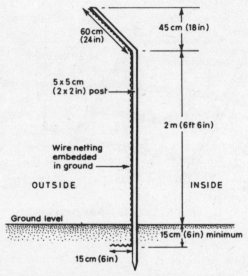

Fig. 7. Fox-proof fencing with safeguards shown against climbing and burrowing by foxes

The wire can be held in position with chestnut posts from which the bark has been removed. The lower part of the posts should be creosoted before use. They are driven into the ground at intervals of 2–3 m (6 ft 6 in–10 ft). The netting is best fixed to the posts with nails bent over rather than staples. Nails are much easier to remove than staples and there is far less chance of damaging the netting if the fence has to be removed. The fence is completed by

running a strand of barbed wire across the top. The strength of
the netting is indicated by the gauge; the lower the number, the
stronger the wire.

The fence should be inspected at regular intervals to ensure that
it is kept in a fox-proof condition. In my experience, foxes will
rarely burrow their way under netting that has been properly
buried in the ground, but a badger will. I remember one occasion
when a badger dug a hole under the wire netting fence of a valuable Rhode Island Red breeding pen. I frequently filled the hole
and the badger dug a fresh one. The game went on for a few days,
but the badger was so persistent that in the end I moved the fence
out of his path.

The gate to the poultry pen should always be self-closing to
guard against the time when someone will leave the gate open and
the birds will get out or the predators will get in. A simple self-
closing solution is to arrange for a heavy weight, such as a piece
of iron piping, to be suspended from a wire that hangs on one
side of the gate-post and is attached to the top of the gate.

Predators always try to enter a poultry pen and they can be
most persistent. The space between the bottom of the gate and the
ground is the most vulnerable place. Keep the gap as small as
possible and make sure that predators cannot burrow underneath. This can be done by placing a line of concrete slabs immediately underneath the gate, or concrete itself, or a piece of
timber as a threshold with wire netting embedded in the ground.
The partition, or the service gate, can be made from 5×5 cm
(2×2 in) deal framing and covered with 5 cm (2 in) mesh wire
netting. Remember to give the wooden parts of the gate a coat of
creosote.

CATCHING CRATE

Handling birds can often be carried out at night, but when it is
necessary to catch birds during the day an easy method is required that does not upset them. Where only a small number of
birds is concerned a small wire-netting covered frame may be

used. The birds are gently driven into a corner of the house with
the help of the frame. It can be about 1×0.75 m (3 ft 3 in $\times$ 2 ft
6 in) and made of 5×4 cm ($2 \times 1\frac{1}{2}$ in) deal, covered with 5 cm
(2 in) mesh wire netting.

A specially-built catching crate is a luxury where only a few
birds are concerned, but an essential with a larger flock. It is
designed to be put immediately outside the pop-hole of the house
and the birds are driven gently into the crate whenever it is
necessary to handle them. A suitable crate is 1.25 m (4 ft) long
and about 0.75 m (2 ft 6 in) wide and 0.6 m (2 ft) deep. The floor
of the crate may be solid and can be made out of exterior-grade
plywood. The framework of the crate can be made of 5×4 cm
($2 \times 1\frac{1}{2}$ in) deal and the sides covered with wire netting or wooden
slats. The top of the crate should have a hinged flap that opens
outward and through which the birds are taken for handling. The
end of the crate placed against the house is arranged as a slide so
that when the birds are in, the slide is lowered.

CATCHING HOOK

A catching hook is easy to make and resembles a small shepherd's
crook; it should be made of strong wire and may be kept hanging
just inside the door of the house (Pl. 14). Catching hooks are of
great value when it is necessary to catch an individual bird. I
knew one man who used an outsized butterfly net for catching
birds and this seemed to work very well.

CARRYING CRATES

Clean crates should be used when collecting or delivering poultry.
A strong cardboard box with ventilation holes made in the sides
and measuring $30 \times 60 \times 30$ cm ($12 \times 24 \times 12$ in) is suitable for
carrying a trio of adult hens and for more bantams. The advantage
of the cardboard box is that it can be burnt after use. Specially-
made carrying boxes may be bought from pet shops, and some

designed for cats rather than poultry are often satisfactory.

The standard carrying crate used by commercial poultry producers is suitable for carrying up to a dozen hens and measures about $31 \times 60 \times 89$ cm ($12\frac{1}{4} \times 24 \times 35$ in). Immediately after use the wooden crate should be thoroughly cleaned and disinfected ready for use again.

PLUCKING BOX

A specially-designed plucking box in which one can sit when plucking chickens is a good idea where a few chickens or ducks have to be plucked each week. The box saves the trouble of clearing up after each bird has been plucked and ensures that the feathers are all kept together (Fig. 8).

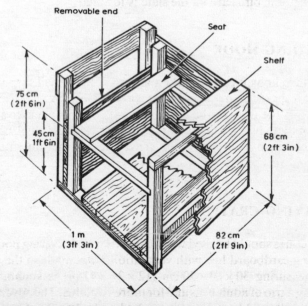

Fig. 8. Plucking box which anyone keen on D-I-Y can easily put together from available bits and pieces

Chapter Three

Establishing and Maintaining a Flock

> Clapping her platter stood plump Bess,
> And all across the green
> Came scampering in on wing and claw,
> Chicken fat and lean;
> Dorking, Spaniard, Cochin China,
> Bantams sleek and small,
> Like feathers blown in a great wind,
> They came at Bessie's call.
>
> Walter de la Mare

Beginning; Incubation; Natural incubation; Artificial incubation; Sexing; Rearing; Floor space; Crowding; Litter; Grass range; Haybox brooders; Handling poultry; Moulting; Lighting; Influence of temperature; Ventilation; Litter management; Egg production; Collection and storage; Management of grass range and land; Land management; Killing and plucking chickens; Value of poultry manure; Health and protection (pests, diseases, etc., in alphabetical order).

BEGINNING

On page 22 I looked briefly at the various ways of starting a flock — point-of-lay pullets, broody hens, day-old chicks and incubated eggs. Now let us look at them more closely, beginning with the egg.

Incubation

The incubation period, that is the time it takes for the hatching eggs to become day-old chicks, varies considerably with the species. The larger the egg, the longer it takes to incubate. Chickens take 21 days, guinea-fowl 26–8, turkeys 28, most ducks 30, Muscovy ducks 33–5 and geese 30–5.

Natural incubation

The reliable broody hen, and for that matter the broody duck, goose, turkey or guinea-hen, is by far the most interesting means of incubation. Unfortunately, finding a broody hen can be very difficult; broodiness is regarded by poultry farmers as an uneconomical character and, as a result, broodiness has almost been bred out of modern laying strains.

The place to find a broody hen is from the flock of one of the poultry fanciers. As a general rule the light Mediterranean breeds, such as Leghorns, tend to be non-broody or unreliable broodies, whereas the heavy breeds, Orpingtons and Sussex, are often excellent. The most persistent broodies are the Silkies.

Broody hens often carry lice which, if not dealt with, will be passed on to the newly hatched chicks. The lice can also walk from the hen to the attendant, but they are quite harmless and will usually die after a few hours. The treatment is to dust the birds under both wings and in the feathers around the vent with an insect powder.

The broody hen is best placed on the nest during the evening to give her the best chance of settling down. Just in case the hen is a little irritable it is a good idea to give her a few china eggs to sit on, to prove herself, before entrusting her with the valuable hatching eggs. The real eggs should be introduced to the broody at night and the bird given sufficient to cover comfortably. Most large broody hens will cover up to fifteen eggs, but the smaller Silkie only eight to ten.

Every day at about the same time the hen should be taken off the nest for some exercise and to allow her to feed and drink. Allow the hen to return to the nest after about twenty minutes. After a few days the hen can be allowed to leave the nest as and when she wishes, but keep an eye on her, for some can be so persistent that they will sit for days without food and water and thus lose condition.

After the hen has been sitting for a week the eggs can be tested for fertility and any infertile eggs removed. The infertile eggs appear absolutely clear when held in front of a light, whereas in the fertile eggs the developing embryo can be seen as a dark, moving blob. An improvised testing box can be made by making a hole of about 2·5 cm (1 in) in a cardboard box about 23 × 15 × 23 cm (9 × 6 × 9 in) and placing this over a strong light (Fig. 9). The eggs are then held against the lighted aperture. This may also be used to check dead embryos after fourteen days (p. 58). Testing eggs in this way is known as 'candling'.

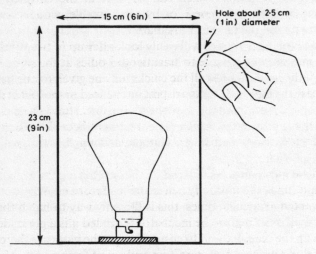

Fig. 9. Testing or candling box for checking eggs

A careful watch should be kept on the condition of the nest and, if the hen accidentally fouls the nest, the droppings and any dirty litter should be removed. Also it is necessary to keep an eye on the soil at the base of the nest. In very dry weather this is apt to dry out unless a little warm water is poured into one corner of the nest from time to time. Very little water is required and this should not come into contact with the eggs.

Once the developing chicks start to peck their way out of the shells, at which stage the eggs are said to be pipping, cover the broody up and leave well alone. Looking at her at this stage can do more harm than good. Wait twenty-four hours or so and the hen will do the job of hatching the chicks and drying them off perfectly well without any outside help. Interfere with the hen and she may walk off in disgust with only half the chicks hatched.

The broody hen should be confined to her coop for the first week after the chicks have hatched, but the young chicks can be allowed out on grass if the weather is suitable. The reason for this is to prevent the broody hen from straying too far away while the chicks are young. The hen can be kept in the coop by wire netting of 8 cm (3 in) mesh or by a removable, wooden-slatted front with the slats 8 cm (3 in) apart.

One large broody hen will easily look after up to twenty chicks so it may be worth while to start two broodies at the same time, then if the hatch is poor all the chicks may be given to one hen. In this case the day-old chicks are best introduced to the hen at dusk. The broody hen may be allowed to run with the young chicks until they are seven to eight weeks old, or younger in the summer, and then used to incubate another batch of eggs.

Artificial incubation

The alternative to a broody hen is an incubator and, where chicks are wanted at specific times, this is the only way to hatch them.

A week or so before the incubator is needed it is a good idea to clean up the machine and to ensure that all the parts are there and in working order. Then start it up and run it for a couple of days to make sure that everything is satisfactory. At this stage the incubator should also be fumigated (p. 81).

Cleanliness is an important management point in artificial incubation and every effort should be made to ensure that the eggs, which are clean when laid, remain clean. Extra attention should be paid to keeping the litter in the nest clean and any dirty litter should be removed immediately.

Hatching eggs should be collected three times a day. Dirty eggs can soon lead to infection in the incubator and, because some eggs will inevitably become dirty, they should be segregated from the clean at the time of collection. The dirty eggs should be cleaned immediately using wire wool or sandpaper. Do not wash hatching eggs as this tends to push any dirt into the pores of the egg.

They should be of a size representative of the breed or strain and should all have sound shells. Any eggs that have cracks, even minute ones, should not generally be used. On the other hand, if the eggs are from a very rare breed or expensive, I would certainly set all the eggs, even if some have hair cracks. In this case all the eggs should be examined and any cracks covered with a piece of Sellotape.

The eggs should be stored in a room that is not too hot and not too cold, and free from draughts. A suitable temperature is between 12 and 15 °C (54 and 59 °F). The eggs may begin to germinate if the temperature exceeds 20 °C (68 °F) and this leads to poor hatching results. As a general rule hatching eggs should not be kept for longer than seven days before setting, to help ensure the highest hatchability. Throughout the period of storage the eggs should be turned at least once daily.

Don't count your chickens before they hatch applies very much to incubation. Under commercial conditions the farmer expects at least eighty chickens to hatch from every hundred eggs set; the hatchability is said to be eighty per cent. On average, half the chicks will be male and half female. A general rule is to set three to four eggs for every adult pullet that one wishes to rear. In the event of too many pullets being reared, the surplus will generally find a ready market. Hatching eggs are rarely available for immediate purchase and it is advisable to book the eggs well ahead. The supplier should provide a guarantee of fertility and this should be a minimum of eighty per cent.

A number of small incubators have been developed that will hold from 25 to 150 eggs. The eggs remain in the same incubator throughout the period of incubation. Usually small incubators are heated electrically and if well managed will give excellent results. On all occasions the management recommendations of the manufacturer should be followed carefully. Some incubators are made with clear plastic tops so that it is possible to see the chicks hatching.

A room in the house may be used for the incubator, but in that event it is necessary to leave a window open at night to ensure sufficient ventilation. A well-insulated out-building will be satisfactory, even if it has an earth floor, so long as fresh air can be provided. An important item to remember is that the rays from the sun should not shine through a window directly on to the incubator. When this happens the temperature inside the incubator can rise rapidly and the eggs may become cooked and the developing chicks killed. A reasonable room temperature inside the incubator room is about 18–20 °C (64–70 °F).

Temperature control is probably the most important single item in incubation management. The required temperature in commercial incubators is almost 38 °C (100 °F). In small machines there is usually a variation in temperature between the top and the bottom of the incubator. Usually the thermometer is suspended just above the eggs and a temperature of 39·5 °C (103 °F) maintained. The important thing is to follow the instructions of the incubator manufacturer.

The temperature of the incubator should be checked every morning and night and recorded, together with any unusual events, so that evidence is available should something go wrong. The hen, when sitting on eggs, is twisting and turning and so the hatching eggs are being regularly turned. Turning is an essential requirement of incubation and, when incubators are used, the hatching eggs should be turned every morning and evening. To ease the task of turning the eggs, a nought may be marked on one side of the egg and a cross on the other. At the same time as turning, the eggs on the inside of the tray should be changed with those on the outside to overcome any variation in temperature that there might be in the different parts of the incubator.

Unless the eggs are regularly turned many, if not all, of the eggs may fail to hatch. After turning, make sure that all the eggs are broad end up if the floor of the incubator tray is fixed at an angle. On the seventh day the eggs should be tested for fertility (p. 54), and on the fourteenth for any embryos that may have died. These are called dead germs, can be seen to have no movement and should be removed. The turning of the eggs should be discontinued after the eighteenth day of incubation.

Follow the advice of the incubator manufacturer as closely as possible. Some incubators have water trays and these should be filled with warm water at the time recommended.

Once the developing chicks start to emerge from their shells you must overcome the temptation to take a look. Cover up the window of the incubator, if necessary, to prevent the early hatched chicks from crowding to the front of the machine. Leave the incubator alone for twenty-four hours. At hatching, it is necessary to pay special attention to temperature because there is a tendency for the incubator temperature to rise during the actual hatching period. This should be expected and any necessary adjustments made.

All the chicks should be dry and fluffy and ready to be removed from the incubator by the end of the twenty-first day of incubation. Sometimes a hatch may take longer and this may be due to continued low temperature. On removing the chicks, examine them and kill any that are malformed. Such chicks may result from improper turning of the hatching eggs or irregular temperature during the period of incubation.

Inadequate ventilation, low temperature and poor management generally may give rise to newly hatched chicks having a wet and bedraggled appearance. If this occurs it is best to seek advice in case the condition is due to the outbreak of some infection. Once all the chicks have been removed from the incubator, the machine should be cleaned and fumigated immediately so that it is ready for use again.

It is often very interesting to be able to identify the offspring of individual hens, especially if you want to go on to pedigree breeding. To be able to do this it is necessary to mark the eggs of the individual hens and put them, either in specially made, wire pedigree boxes or in muslin bags, for the last three days of incubation. The muslin bags are the cheaper method and eggs from one particular hen are put in one bag, which should be made to hold from three to six eggs. The muslin bag is then tied and labelled, making sure that the label is secure and that it gives all the details required.

On hatching, the chicks of the individual hens are removed from the bags and identified by a small metal tag, called a wing band, fixed on their wings. An alternative method of marking is to make a small cut in the web of the foot.

SEXING

Chicks that are bought as hatched can usually be sexed by general appearance at from four to ten weeks. The light breeds of chickens as a rule can be sexed at an earlier age than the heavy breeds. The cockerels have larger and redder combs than the pullets and, in the case of the light breeds, the tails of the males appear before those of the females. The feathers on the backs of the heavy-breed males do not grow as quickly as those of the females and often their backs appear stubby due to the slowly growing feathers.

Hybrid chickens are usually sexed and divided into males and females at a day old so that it is possible to buy day-old chicks of the sex required. In the case of the popular laying strains only the females are reared; the males are so light that they are not acceptable for meat production.

Many of the popular hybrid strains may be sexed either by their down colour or by the length of their rudimentary wing feathers. This means of sexing is known as auto-sexing. When two distinct breeds are mated and it is possible to distinguish the sex of the offspring at a day old by their appearance, they are said to be sex-linked.

Sexing by down colour is a feature of a number of the brown-shelled strains of poultry. The pullet chicks are predominantly reddish brown in down colour, whereas the males are white or off white. Feather sexing, based on the length of certain feathers at a day old, is common among the meat-type chickens. The flight feathers are of two types: the primary and the covert feathers. In the male day-olds of a feather-sexing strain, both types of feathers are about the same length, or sometimes the primary feathers are a little shorter than the coverts. On the other hand, the rudimentary primary feathers of the females are distinctly longer than the wing covert feathers (Fig. 10).

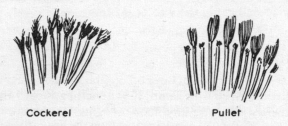

Cockerel   Pullet

Fig. 10. Sexing of day-old chicks by length of covert feathers, those in the female being longer

REARING

Considerable care and attention is necessary to ensure that the young chicks have the best possible start in life. The brooding accommodation should be prepared ready for use at least a couple of days before the chicks arrive. Make sure that everything is ready and in working order. The day before the chicks (both bought or home hatched) are due, switch on the heating, fill up the food hoppers and also the water troughs. Always have everything clean; the floor on which the chicks are to run, and all the equipment, should be scrubbed with hot water and washing soda.

Generally artificial heat is required until the birds are six to eight weeks old. Overheating should be avoided but it is a good idea to have a reserve of heat so that the birds can warm up quickly whenever they want, just as they would under a mother hen.

Electric brooders are generally the most satisfactory for use by the domestic poultry keeper. Compared with oil-heated brooders the fire risk is low and another advantage is that they are very convenient to use. The most satisfactory for the small-scale producer is the so-called electric hen, which is designed to allow the height of the brooder to be adjusted as the birds grow and is suitable to rear up to a hundred chicks.

Another simple brooder is the hanging infra-red or electric lamp and this is usually cheaper to buy than the electric hen, but the running costs will be slightly higher. The lamp is merely suspended over the chicks. Arrangement should be made to prevent the young chicks from straying too far from the source of heat during the early days. This can be done by making a circular 'fence' of cardboard, wire netting or hardboard and placing it immediately underneath the lamp. If wire netting is used make sure that there will not be any floor draughts. At the start the circle for a hundred chicks can be 1·25 m (4 ft) in diameter. After a few days the circle should be extended and finally removed when the chicks are about ten days old (Fig. 11).

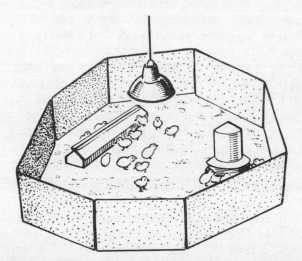

Fig. 11. Brooder showing surround to prevent draughts

Care should be taken to ensure that the chicks under an infra-red brooder, or under an electric light bulb, are not under- or overheated. Ideally the chicks should be in a circle, not huddled immediately beneath the lamp. If you find them huddled together it can indicate the birds are too cold or are unhealthy.

Floor space
Make sure the chicks have sufficient floor space, but not too much. A hundred chicks will require 4·65 sq m (50 sq ft) up to four weeks, and 9·3 sq m (100 sq ft) up to eight weeks of age.

Most chicks arrive from the hatchery in boxes with divisions that hold twenty-five birds. Whenever possible collect the chicks from the hatchery. Chicks in boxes standing in draughty houses can soon become chilled, particularly if they have been im-properly packed. The chicks should be unpacked with care, in-dividually inspected and placed under the source of heat. Make sure that the brooder has been warmed up to prevent the possi-bility of the chicks becoming chilled. Visit the brooder every few hours during the first twenty-four to make sure that everything is working well. If the chicks have travelled a long way, allow them food and water immediately they arrive, even if this means switching on the light or camping gas lamp so they can see.

Check that the chicks are sleeping in a circle under the brooder with plenty of space in the centre. When they huddle together im-mediately under the brooder because they are not warm enough, they are likely to become chilled in the early hours of the morning when the temperature falls. Young chicks of all species can easily become chilled during their early life and this can result from a number of management faults. Draughts at floor level are a par-ticular hazard and allowing the chicks too much floor space can also lead to trouble. Overheating as well as underheating can also lead to losses.

Crowding
Chicks sometimes run into corners of their house and pile up, one on the other, and the result can be heavy losses. Paradoxically, it is frequently the strongest chicks that are lost because they

push their way under the others. Often the reason for the crowding is not clear and in many cases the dead birds are not found until the morning. To overcome this problem the corners of the house should be rounded off with some wire netting. A good idea is to make some simple triangular frames out of some 5 × 2·5 cm (2 × 1 in) battening and to cover the frames with 2·5 cm (1 in) wire netting. One frame can be placed in each corner. The frame should be about 75 cm (30 in) on all sides. An alternative, but one that is not so good, is to place a sack of hay in each corner (Fig. 12).

Fig. 12. Corner of poultry house showing triangular frames to keep chicks from crowding into corners and suffocating

Crowding can occur at any age if birds are suddenly frightened, although the chance of this occurring with mature birds is not very great. The age at which most losses occur is between three and nine weeks of age. A particularly dangerous time is when birds are moved from one house to another, especially among chickens that are not used to perching. Look at the birds several times during the day that they are moved and make a special visit at night.

Whenever young chicks huddle together the matter should be investigated; the chicks may be too cold, there may be a draught, or the huddling may indicate the onset of some malady. Prompt action may be the means of avoiding some serious losses.

Litter
The young chicks need dry, clean and sweet litter at all times; sawdust, soft-wood shavings, wheat chaff or peat moss are all satisfactory. Wet or damp patches of litter should be removed immediately and replaced with clean litter, as part of the disease prevention programme. A hundred chicks will generally need about 100 kg (about 2 cwt) of wood shavings to last for the brooding period of up to eight weeks.

Grass range
Young chicks may, if the weather is suitable, be allowed access to good quality grass from the first few days, but it is generally far more convenient to rear them intensively for the first four to six weeks. The range on which the young chicks run should be selected with care and the land should be ground on which other poultry have not ranged for at least a year.

At whatever age the chicks are finally allowed on to range they should be kept to a small area near the entrance of their house for a day or two. Wire netting may be used to make a small run, or a wire-netting cage can be made. Once the birds are used to their surroundings they can be given unrestricted range; but think twice about it if there is any danger that Master Reynard or the neighbour's dogs may pay a call.

Until the birds are eight to ten weeks old they should be visited frequently throughout the day to make sure that all is well. At the first sign of rain it is usually necessary to drive the birds back into their house, otherwise there is a danger of their becoming wet through and subsequently dying from having become chilled.

Haybox brooders
Chickens can be reared without artificial heat from four weeks of age with the help of a haybox brooder. Brooders of this type can

be made for use inside a building or as part of a fold unit that is moved to a new patch of land every day.

A haybox brooder suitable for twenty-five to thirty birds, being reared inside a house, is simple to make. Start with a box about 90 × 90 cm (36 × 36 in) and sides about 40 cm (16 in). A sacking screen is arranged to fit over the top and hang down just above the backs of the chickens. A bag of hay or feathers, or an old blanket is placed on top to conserve the natural animal heat. A few holes 2·5 cm (1 in) in diameter should be drilled in the sides of the box for ventilation. Instead of wood, the sides can be made of two layers of wire netting with hay packed between. The front of the box is covered with a curtain, cut into sections, to allow the chicks in and out to feed and drink; for the first few days the run can be not more than 1 m (3 ft 3 in) long and after that they may have as much room as liked up to 2 m (6 ft 6 in).

HANDLING POULTRY

Regular observation and handling of birds are essential in good poultry keeping. All stock should be handled regularly — every month — and the less satisfactory birds removed and killed. The practice of handling and removing birds is known as culling and the individuals removed are culls.

Individual birds can be caught during the day with the help of a catching hook. Birds are far less excited if they are handled after dark and at this time they can be lifted off their perches gently, without upsetting them and without their trying to escape. Handling can be carried out during the day with use of a catching crate (p. 49).

One of the best ways of handling a bird is to pick it up with your right hand over its back, at the same time grasping the wing and the leg. The bird is then placed in the palm of the left hand with the head resting on your arm. The legs are held between the fingers, but remember to keep two fingers between the legs. This is most important when handling birds in lay, for if you grasp the two legs together the abdomen may be accidentally squeezed. The bird is examined by gripping the legs lightly with the left hand and balancing it with the right.

Look at its head, eyes and throat, and the base of the feathers around the vent for lice, which should be treated if necessary. At the same time examine the vent for any abnormality such as signs of sores, which might be vent gleet (p. 86). The general body condition of the bird should be noted and also run the hand over its crop. Any birds without food in their crops have either been given insufficient for their needs or are showing early signs of ill health.

The onset of egg production is indicated by the reddening up of the comb and wattles and eggs can usually be expected within a few weeks. The aim should be to bring the birds into lay at about twenty weeks and to have them in their permanent houses before production actually starts. If the pullets have to be moved when they are actually in lay, do so carefully, a few at a time. Look at the birds at dusk and any that are not perching should be lifted and settled gently on the perches.

Checking whether the birds are actually in lay is simple, once the rudiments have been mastered. Birds with bright-red combs and wattles are probably in production and this can be confirmed by feeling the two pelvic bones. These thin bones lie almost on either side of the vent. The pelvic bones of birds in lay are well apart, a space about two or three fingers' wide. The birds that are out of lay have the pelvic bones close together. The skin round the vent is very moist, soft and pliable in the bird in lay, but tends to be dry and, in many breeds, yellowish in appearance in non-laying birds. Those that are out of lay when the rest are laying well should be considered as possible table birds, unless there is a good reason for retaining them in the flock.

Any bird that shows signs of ill health should be moved from the flock immediately and put in an isolation pen for treatment. Prolonged treatment is seldom worth while. If infectious disease is suspected, veterinary advice should be sought and all visits to and from neighbours should be stopped until the problems have been resolved. This is a wise precaution aimed at preventing the spread of disease.

MOULTING

Laying chickens that have not been subject to light control generally moult in late summer or autumn as the days begin to draw in. As a rule, laying birds go out of lay during the moult and males lose the inclination to mate. In general terms it can be said that the poor producers moult earlier and the better ones later. The pullets that moult after laying well into the winter are usually the best ones to keep for breeding purposes. A few birds will continue to lay throughout the moulting period; in these cases the moult is usually very gradual and prolonged. The time taken by birds to complete the moult and to recommence egg production varies from six to twelve weeks.

The pattern of moulting is regular and the birds begin by losing their feathers in this sequence: the head, followed by the neck, the breast and, finally, the wings and tail feathers. The time of the year in which the birds are hatched has an influence on the time at which moulting occurs. Laying birds hatched from October to February will generally moult, sometimes only a partial neck moult, in the early autumn. The earlier-hatched pullets may lay a hundred or so eggs before moulting, whereas the late-hatched birds only about forty eggs.

LIGHTING

The effect of the natural increase in day length in spring and the decrease in autumn is very marked on chicks hatched in December and January. They come into lay early and in the autumn tend to go out of production, providing few winter eggs. With birds on free range it is possible to alter the lighting pattern by arranging a combination of natural and artificial light. A 25- to 40-watt bulb will usually be sufficient for a small poultry house with up to a dozen birds.

The pattern of light which the pullets receive during their rear-

ing period up to twenty weeks of life can influence the following:
1. The age at which egg production starts.
2. The liveweight at the start of laying.
3. The amount of food eaten.
4. The number of eggs laid.
5. The size of eggs laid.
6. The incidence of feather pecking.

The best time of year to hatch chicks to avoid the worst effects of the lighting pattern is between March and September. Artificial lighting may not be required at all with March-hatched birds. On the other hand, birds hatched at the turn of the year and in January will usually come into lay about five weeks earlier than those hatched in July. Early egg production—fifteen to sixteen weeks of age instead of twenty—results in birds of very low body weight, the production of small eggs and increased chances of losses of birds from prolapsus, eversion of the oviduct.

The easiest method of avoiding these disadvantages with winter-hatched birds is to give them some artificial light so that the total light provided gives a fourteen-hour day up to twenty weeks.

The most convenient way to provide light is by suspending an ordinary electric light bulb at a height of about 2 m (6 ft 6 in) above floor level. A 25- or 40-watt bulb will be sufficient for a house of 10 sq m (108 sq ft). There is no advantage in using coloured lights, in fact such lights are a disadvantage in that they use more electricity to give the same amount of light because the colour reduces the intensity.

Feather pecking rarely occurs with birds reared on range but frequently causes trouble with birds reared intensively. The most simple means of combating the vice is to reduce the intensity of the light inside the house by hanging sacks over the windows and by using a lower wattage bulb in electric lights.

INFLUENCE OF TEMPERATURE

Poultry do not thrive during periods of very hot weather and one of the reasons is that they do not have any sweat glands. Keeping cool can be a problem and one way in which they can help themselves is by flicking water over themselves. The water troughs during the hot months of the year should enable the birds' wattles and combs to become a little wet when they drink; this is a great help.

Everything possible should be done to help the birds keep cool. Shade is very important. Make sure that the sun cannot shine directly into the birds' houses. Increase the insulation in the roof of the poultry building by putting a good layer of straw on the roof until the hot weather has passed. The water trough should be in the shade and not in the blazing sun, and a cool water supply provided, even if this means making one or two extra trips to the birds during the day.

For birds kept in an urban area, where range is restricted, particular attention is necessary during a summer scorcher. A good idea is to provide a wire-netting screen to the door of the house so that it can be left open. Any windows should be kept open and an additional help is a blanket hung over the door or window so that it can be hosed down with water two or three times during the heat of the day.

VENTILATION

Birds of all kinds require plenty of fresh air at all times, but it should be fresh air without draughts. The principle upon which natural ventilation of a poultry house is based is that the heat produced by the birds rises, to be replaced by cooler fresh air.

One of the snags of natural ventilation is that during the winter months there may be little difference in temperature between the inside and the outside of the house, but as a general rule the small-scale poultry keeper should allow plenty of room in the house so that ventilation problems, particularly in an open-fronted house, do not arise.

LITTER MANAGEMENT

The floor of the house should be well covered with litter and the aim is to keep the litter dry at all times. Birds love to scratch and at times to have dust baths, but they cannot do so if the litter becomes a matted carpet of droppings. Apart from that, wet and soggy litter can provide just the right conditions for an outbreak of disease.

The most absorbent litter is peat moss. However, the use of peat moss is not environmentally friendly because it is a non-renewable resource and cannot be recommended. Alternatives are available including wood shavings and shredded paper. At the end of the season poultry litter makes very valuable fertilizer for the garden.

Pinewood shavings, sawdust or chaffed straw, to a depth of 15 cm (6 in) also make a first-class litter. Care must be taken to ensure that the litter has not at some time become wet or musty. Musty litter can precipitate an outbreak of a fungal disease, a form of pneumonia, known as aspergillosis (see p. 76). Hardwood shavings are not satisfactory as litter and should not be used. Another point to remember: shavings and sawdust from timber that has been treated with an insecticide should also be avoided.

Newly hatched chicks that have not yet become accustomed to eating may tend to eat sawdust if it is used as the sole litter. It is best, therefore, to cover the sawdust with paper bags for the first few days of the chick's life. The golden rule of litter management is to remove any damp or wet patches of litter the moment they are spotted and replace with fresh litter.

EGG PRODUCTION

Profitable poultry keeping demands that records of performance should be kept and it may be helpful to have a knowledge of the jargon used by commercial producers of eggs and table poultry.

In the case of egg production the number of eggs laid is usually expressed as a percentage of the number of birds in the flock. Thus if the flock consists of ten laying birds which have laid an average of eight eggs daily for a week, the flock is said to have averaged eighty per cent production; this can be calculated on either a daily or weekly basis—weekly is more usual.

Once egg production begins, the young pullets usually lay more and more eggs daily until reaching a 'peak' of ninety per cent or more at about twenty-six to thirty weeks of age. The flocks hold their peak for several weeks and then production gradually falls, reaching fifty to sixty per cent production by the end of the laying year.

Age is an important influence on the number of eggs laid. Generally a bird will lay more eggs in the first year than in subsequent years. Production can be expected to fall by about ten to twelve per cent with every year of age. As a rule of thumb, laying chickens should not be kept for more than two laying seasons, except for sentimental reasons.

Production also depends on the strain of bird. The breeders of hybrid strains publish charts which give the potential production of their strains. There can be considerable variation between the best and the least satisfactory. Some lay a lot of eggs, some are specially noted for their egg size or shell colour and some are very efficient in their conversion of food into eggs.

Food conversion, usually written f.c., is a good guide to performance. In respect of egg production, the f.c. represents the amount of feed consumed per kilo or per dozen eggs. A reasonable f.c. for laying birds fed on bought foods is 2·75–3·0:1, which means a total of 2·75–3·0 kg of food for every kilo of eggs produced. Some birds have an efficiency as good as 2·5:1.

Collection and storage of eggs

Eggs are clean at the time of laying and every effort should be made to keep them in perfect condition. They are best collected two or three times daily and stored in a cool room. Put them directly into the egg trays from which they will be used, to cut out any unnecessary handling and to avoid cracked eggs. Eggs soon lose their fresh quality if improperly stored. The best storage place is the refrigerator, but not at too cold a temperature. A room temperature of 5–10 °C (41–50 °F) is considered the best, but in not too dry an atmosphere.

Infertile eggs, that is eggs from hens that are not running with a cockerel, keep better than fertile eggs. The porous nature of the eggshell means that eggs can quickly pick up taints if stored near such things as paraffin, onions or garlic, for example. Another cause of tainted eggs is the use of poor-quality fish scraps or low-grade fish meal.

One of the chores when dealing with chickens that have the freedom to range wherever they wish is that of actually finding where they have laid their eggs. An interesting way of collecting eggs is to train a dog. Basil was such a dog and had been trained to perfection by my friend. He was a lovely golden cocker spaniel and not only would he find the nest but also bring the eggs back to the house one at a time, then wag his tail until someone noticed and rewarded him with a thank-you pat. On the day of the annual church fete, Basil surpassed himself. The daughters of the house were in charge of the stand with the raffle prizes, which included a basket of a dozen large brown eggs. Just as the fete was about to be opened, with all the celebrities in line, Basil appeared wagging his tail furiously. When he reached the vicar's wife he deposited one of the prize eggs at her feet, much to the delight of the spectators and the cheers of the children.

Cleaning eggs
Dirty eggs should be cleaned immediately after collection with the help of some wire wool or sandpaper. Eggs should not be washed except in special circumstances; it may result in the development of moulds inside the eggs. Eggs that have been washed do not keep as well as unwashed eggs. Some eggs will get so dirty that they have to be washed; the best way is to use hot water and just a little detergent. Wash, rinse and dry the eggs as quickly as possible and never leave them soaking in water. After washing, some of the eggs may still be too badly stained for use as boiled eggs or for sale; these should be used for cooking and not stored.

MANAGEMENT OF GRASS RANGE AND LAND

The houses of birds on unrestricted free range should preferably be moved their length once a week to prevent the birds from ruining the grass immediately round the house. It is important not to move the house more than its length for, if it is moved too far, the birds will gather round the spot where the house used to be rather than going to the new spot in the evening. The result is a tempting dish for the fox and a lot of trouble for the owner in trying to catch the birds and return them to their house.

Whenever the range house has to be moved a distance from one position to another the birds should be confined to the area round the house, by wire netting, for the first few days to get them used to their new surroundings. The first time they are given freedom to range, let them out for only an hour or so before dusk.

Running too many birds on range can soon lead to problems. The number kept will depend on the type of soil and the vegetation. More birds can be run on light sandy soils than on heavy clay such as I have in my part of Sussex. An average of 125 chickens or ducks a hectare (50 birds an acre) is generally sufficient. Turkeys need more room and 75 a hectare (25 an acre) is satisfactory. Geese tend to be rather more messy than other poultry and 25 a hectare (10 an acre) is ample.

Land management

Poultry running over grassland in reasonable numbers provide some valuable fertilizer but, because it is not properly balanced, the quality of the grass will deteriorate unless appropriate action is taken. Poultry manure tends to increase the acidity of the land and the soil may become deficient in potash. To keep the grass in good condition it is essential to dress the land once a year with carbonate of lime, at the rate of 1,000 kg a hectare (1 ton an acre). The soil should be checked for potash and, if necessary, a potash fertilizer applied.

Small runs on which birds have to spend a considerable time

need special care and attention. Overstocking of the land should always be avoided, for once the grass has been ruined it is very difficult to get it to grow again and the run is useless for poultry. Land that has been newly planted should not be stocked until the young grass has had time to become fully established.

Once a year runs should be limed as a matter of routine and any bare patches treated with a mixture of copper sulphate and sand to eliminate worms and slugs, as part of the disease-prevention programme (p. 76).

Stinging nettles are a frequent problem and quickly appear on any piece of land which poultry have denuded of grass. Nettles thrive on an acid soil and are very difficult to eliminate. Regular cutting of the stalks helps to exhaust the root stocks of the nettles.

Young chicks may be allowed out on grass from a day old, but the more common practice is to rear them indoors up to about four weeks. The land should not have had other poultry grazing on it for at least twelve months before being used by the chicks. The ground can, of course, be grazed by other stock, and sheep will keep the grass down to the lawn-like state preferred by chicks. The use of poor quality grassland by young chicks can soon lead to problems with impacted crops and intestines and possibly worm infection.

Where land is very limited it is best to arrange for each house to have two runs that can be used alternately. The more run that can be provided the better, but a minimum is 8–12 sq m a bird (10–15 sq yd) in each of the alternate runs.

One of the main problems of the semi-intensive system is that the ground, particularly near the house, may soon lose all the grass and the concentration of droppings tends to make the area foul. The land is then said to be poultry sick and can soon become a health hazard. One way to reduce the risk is to surround each house with a bed of cinders or gravel up to about a width of 2 m (6 ft 6 in). This area can then be hosed down from time to time and replaced whenever necessary.

KILLING AND PLUCKING CHICKENS

For the domestic producer the most suitable method of killing poultry is by dislocation of the neck. The neck is broken so that a cavity is left between the head and the neck into which the blood drains. The best way to learn the technique is by watching an experienced person demonstrate it.

Birds to be killed should be allowed clean drinking water right up to the last minute, but grain feeding should be discontinued the day before and mash four to six hours before killing.

Plucking should be carried out immediately, and again the best means of learning is from a practical demonstration. The final preparation of the bird for the oven is not too difficult but it is necessary to maintain a very high standard of hygiene.

The whole subject of killing, plucking and trussing is dealt with in the Ministry of Agriculture Advisory Leaflet 428 entitled 'Preparation and Trussing of Poultry for Market'. The leaflet can be obtained free from the Ministry and contains an excellent series of fifteen photographs of chicken-trussing, ready for the oven.

VALUE OF POULTRY MANURE

Poultry litter and manure, properly used, can be a most valuable supplement to the garden. The manure should be dried before use or incorporated in the compost heap. Laying birds produce 85–115 g (3–4 oz) of fresh manure daily, so a flock of ten will provide 305–460 kg (6–9 cwt) of valuable fertilizer every year. The fresh manure contains about seventy per cent of moisture, which must be removed before use in the garden. Poultry manure is high in nitrogen, rich in phosphate, but low in potash. In terms of fertilizers, the annual output of manure from ten hens is equal to: 50 kg (110 lb) of sulphate of ammonia, 38 kg (84 lb) of superphosphate and 10 kg (22 lb) of thirty per cent potash salts.

Fresh poultry manure can be dried off by sprinkling with superphosphate. Such a practice tends to reduce the smell of the droppings and 28 g (1 oz) of superphosphate will be sufficient for the droppings of ten birds. The manure is best stored under cover and after a few weeks the treated manure will become very dry and friable and suitable for use in the garden.

Poultry manure must be dealt with properly and regularly and on no account just left outside exposed to the weather. Rain will quickly turn the manure heap into a boggy mess, vermin will be attracted, flies will be provided with a good breeding ground and a health and environmental problem will soon arise.

HEALTH AND PROTECTION

Good management, in all its forms, is the best way to maintain healthy birds: well-balanced diet, to build up resistance to disease; no overcrowding or overstocking of land, to reduce the possibility of feather pecking or cannibalism and problems with intestinal worms and other diseases; and a high standard of cleanliness, as special safeguard against infection.

Outbreaks of disease are bound to occur from time to time, despite a high standard of management, because some diseases are airborne and others are carried by wild birds and rodents. Rapid diagnosis and treatment of disease is most important and, if there is any doubt at all, call in veterinary advice.

The main aim with every poultry unit, however small, is to keep disease at bay, and one of the safeguards is to make the minimum number of visits to other poultry units. On occasions when a neighbour persuades you to look after and handle some of his birds, remember to wash your hands afterwards. Do not go straight from other birds to handle your own, for this is one sure way of introducing trouble. One very practical and essential means of keeping down disease is to clean and disinfect every poultry house whenever it becomes empty.

Aspergillosis
Sometimes called brooder pneumonia, aspergillosis may cause

heavy losses in young growing chicks. The birds may appear unsteady on their feet and show nervous symptoms. The disease is often associated with the use of mouldy sawdust or damp hay that has been used for litter. Commonly, the fungus *Aspergillus fumigatus* is involved, but other species of fungi may sometimes be present.

Beak trimming
Beak trimming, which is carried out to reduce losses from feather pecking and cannibalism, should only be performed as a last resort, when it is clear that more suffering would be caused if the beaks of the birds were not trimmed. Whenever it becomes necessary, trimming should be carried out by a skilled craftsman or under his supervision.

Bad trimming is likely to result from the faulty use of poorly designed equipment, or from a failure to understand the structure of the beak and to appreciate that the soft sensitive tissues underlying the corny covering may not easily recover from severe trimming.

Trimming is generally carried out with an electrically heated knife, which should be hot enough and sharp enough to make a clean wound and at the same time cauterize it at a controlled temperature. A modern machine will also have a guide bar retaining the beak so that an excessive length cannot be cut from it.

Blood tests
Blood of breeding birds may be tested to identify any carriers of *Salmonella pullorum*, the cause of pullorum disease, and of certain other salmonella-disease-carrying organisms. The testing is usually undertaken by the Animal Health Division of the Ministry of Agriculture.

Cannibalism
Improper feeding, overcrowding, insufficient food-hopper space, all of which add up to poor or indifferent management, may precipitate an outbreak of feather pecking followed by cannibalism. Poultry reared on range or in grass pens are rarely affected. Badly

pecked birds should be isolated from other members of the flock and the injured parts given liberal coats of Stockholm tar or a proprietary preparation. To prevent recurrence of the vice, check all management details; if the birds are being reared intensively consider reducing the light intensity. Really stubborn cases of feather pecking, if one or two birds have developed the habit, may be overcome by fitting the ringleaders with plastic blinkers or spectacles. Only blinkers of a type unlikely to cause the bird to injure itself when freeing itself from entanglement should be used.

Coccidiosis

This is characterized by blood-stained droppings and general poor growth in young birds. Mortality may be high unless prompt action is taken. Several excellent drugs are now available and these can be included in food or drinking water for prevention or cure. Where coccidiosis is thought to be a problem, the best method of rearing is to use a bought food during the first eight weeks and make sure that it contains a suitable coccidiostat. After an outbreak, spray the house, equipment and land near the house with a spray of ten per cent solution of household ammonia.

Depluming mites

Depluming mites live constantly on the birds and, in addition to causing irritation, may cause the skin to become red and the feathers, particularly those in the region of the neck and head, to break. Depluming mites can be responsible for loss of condition and poor results generally. The mites may not be easy to eradicate and all the birds in the group should be treated, individual birds being dusted or sprayed with a suitable pesticide. The birds should be inspected ten to fourteen days after the first treatment and a second application may be necessary. In stubborn cases the birds should be dipped in a suitable insecticide using tepid water. They can be held by the wings and lowered into the solution. After removal, the feathers may be dried, using a hair-dryer if necessary. The best time to carry out this treatment is in the morning to give plenty of time for drying. Make sure that the birds are thoroughly wet before they are removed from the solution and then follow the recommendations carefully. Under no circumstances should birds under two months of age be treated.

Disinfection of houses

Once poultry are given the use of a house it becomes infected and, in continuous use, there is a progressive build-up of microbes which can sometimes result in sickness and poor productivity. It is for this reason that all poultry houses should be thoroughly cleaned and disinfected after each batch of birds and then left empty for at least two weeks.

The first stage is to spray the inside of the house and the litter with water and disinfectant or detergent to lay the dust because dust is not only objectionable to work in but also it can be blown downwind and sometimes infect other poultry. The litter is then removed to a compost heap well away from the other poultry.

The second stage is to scrape any parts of the house where droppings have become caked and then scrub the house with hot water and washing soda. A cupped double-handful of ordinary washing soda will be sufficient for 11 l ($2\frac{1}{2}$ galls) of water.

Finally, the inside of the house should be sprayed with a suitable disinfectant solution and, in the event of there having been an outbreak of disease, it may be necessary to fumigate the building (p. 81). It is important that the disinfectant used is one that has been approved by the Ministry of Agriculture.

Disposal of dead birds

It is always a problem to know just what to do with birds that die, for if they are left lying around they become a disease hazard, encourage vermin and also give rise to unpleasant smells. Dead birds can be buried, but make sure the hole is deep, or the body may be uncovered by a fox or be reached by rats. Commercial poultry keepers either burn the dead birds in an incinerator or slip them into a specially built disposal pit.

Dubbing

The practice of removing part of the comb of a chicken is known as dubbing and the object is to reduce the risk of frostbite for birds whose combs are very large. Dubbing is also carried out sometimes to hide malformed combs, such as side sprigs, which may be looked upon as a fault in some exhibition birds.

The best age to dub is at a day old for at this time the task is a simple one of snipping off the rudimentary comb with some curved scissors. I do not recommend dubbing and certainly it should not be carried out on birds over seventy-two hours old. The dubbing of older birds, where this proves to be necessary, should only be carried out on veterinary advice and by a skilled craftsman.

Fleas and bugs

These are seldom a problem on a well-managed poultry unit. Fleas, however, can be introduced to poultry by sparrows and starlings, and bugs by pigeons. The fleas may be found on the birds or in the litter, particularly in the nest-boxes. Bugs attack the birds at night and engorge themselves with blood. They hide in cracks and crevices of the poultry house during the day.

Individual birds may be treated by dusting or spraying with a suitable pesticide and the birds should be inspected ten to fourteen days later and treated again if necessary. The fleas and bugs can only be eradicated from the poultry house by thorough cleaning and spraying.

Fowl pest (see Newcastle disease)

Fox precautions

The nursery story of the fox stealing the old grey goose must certainly have been written from bitter experience. Most free-range poultry keepers have their own stories of losing birds to the fox and often the losses take place in broad daylight. The fox is, in many parts of the country and now even in towns, the biggest enemy of the free-range enthusiast and of those who keep their birds on the semi-intensive system.

In fox-infested country the only way to prevent the fox from enjoying a free meal of one of the birds is to shut them up every evening and to provide fox-proof fences to the pen. This is much easier said than done. The pens can be shut up every evening at dusk, but one can be almost certain that the very evening when dusk arrives unnoticed the fox will decide to make a call. The house itself must also be securely made; a hungry fox will soon gain entrance to a rickety house.

Fox-proof fencing is another problem. It is rather expensive but is the only way if you decide to leave the birds, particularly waterfowl, out at night (Fig. 7).

Fumigating

Where there has been an outbreak of disease or where a second-hand house has been bought, the cleaning-up process should always be completed by fumigating the house. The most convenient method of fumigation is with formalin, by spraying with either an aerosol or generator. An alternative is to use 128 g ($4\frac{1}{2}$ oz) of formalin poured on to 85 g (3 oz) of potassium permanganate for every 2·83 cu m (100 cu ft) of house space. Considerable care is necessary when carrying out fumigation by this method and on no account should anyone be allowed into the house unless they are wearing a respirator.

The container for the permanganate should be deep sided and this should be put inside another receptacle to minimize problems if the contents boil over. The containers should be set on brick bases in wooden-floored houses and the right quantity of permanganate put in them. The operator should then stand outside the house, pour the formalin on top of the permanganate and close the door immediately. The door should be locked and a notice fixed on it to prevent anyone from accidently opening the door. This, however, is not really a do-it-yourself job and it is better left to an expert.

Gaping

Gape worms may become a problem with birds kept in small pens or on the semi-intensive system. Whenever young birds stretch their heads and necks forward with their beaks constantly opening, gape worms should be suspected. To ascertain the cause, veterinary advice should be sought.

Green droppings

The droppings of poultry often indicate that the birds are not in first-class condition. The droppings should normally be well formed with a whitish cap. Green droppings should call for immediate action for they could indicate an outbreak of fowl pest (including Newcastle disease); veterinary advice is needed.

Lameness

Lameness, leg weakness and paralysis in young birds may indicate an error in management or the presence of disease. It is impossible to be sure of the cause of leg weakness without veterinary advice. Swollen hocks may be due to a deficiency of Vitamin D, as in rickets. Bandy legs may indicate a mineral imbalance in the diet. Musty litter may result in lameness due to an outbreak of aspergillosis. Lameness in the later stages of the growing period may result from an outbreak of Marek's disease, against which most commercial egg-producing pullets are now vaccinated at a day old before they leave the hatchery.

Lice

Lice are one of the most frequently found skin parasites of chickens and are often present in small numbers without apparently doing very much harm. The lice lay their eggs at the base of the feathers, particularly in the somewhat moist area near the vent, where they may be seen as greyish spots. The eggs hatch within ten to fourteen days.

Individual birds may be treated by dusting or spraying with a suitable insecticide. The product should be specially applied to the feathers near the vent and under the wing. Often one treatment is sufficient, for most pesticides remain on the feathers long enough to kill any lice that hatch from the eggs. If a pyrethrum product is used, however, a second treatment should be given after ten days.

Marek's disease

At one time Marek's disease was included in disease complex

known as fowl paralysis and was responsible for very heavy losses among growing pullets, particularly near point of lay, and older birds. Nowadays the use of a vaccine has largely overcome the problem. The vaccination is best conducted at the hatchery at day old. Whenever day-old pullets are ordered, it is wise to ask for them to be vaccinated against Marek's disease before despatch.

Newcastle disease

Certain diseases of animals are considered to be so serious that they are known as the notifiable diseases. Newcastle disease, which is one form of fowl pest, is one such disease, and it is an obligation on all poultry keepers that if the presence of Newcastle disease is suspected it must be reported without delay to a police officer. The police notify the Ministry of Agriculture and a veterinarian from the Ministry carries out the necessary inspection. Symptoms which may lead to the suspicion that Newcastle disease is present include the appearance of green droppings and a sudden fall in egg production coupled with signs of colds. The other form of fowl pest, fowl plague, is rare.

Pinioning

Pinioning, de-winging, wing notching or tendon severing are sometimes practised to reduce the effects of flightiness, often to prevent the birds from flying away. It must be emphasized that the official Codes of Welfare state quite specifically that this should not be undertaken. On those occasions when it is necessary to prevent the birds from flying, the flight feathers of one wing may be clipped.

Red mites and northern fowl mites

Red mites live in the cracks and crevices of the poultry house, particularly under the ends of the perches. At night the mites crawl out on to the birds where they feed by sucking their blood. The mites can be the cause of anaemia in young stock and also may be responsible for poor egg production. The mites may sometimes be recognized by the salt-and-pepper markings at the end of the perches.

Northern fowl mites differ from red mites in that they live constantly on the birds. These mites can do just as much damage as red mites but can be more difficult to eradicate.

A constant watch should be kept because mites can be introduced by wild birds, particularly starlings and sparrows. Individual birds may be treated by dusting or spraying with a suitable insecticide. A second treatment should be given about ten days after the first. Such treatment, however, will catch only those mites that are actually on the birds. To destroy the mites in the house it is necessary to lay the dust by spraying the house and litter with water containing a detergent, to remove the litter well away from the house and, if only a small quantity, to burn it. The house should then be scrubbed and disinfected thoroughly. Finally, the wooden parts of the house should be given a coat of creosote.

Rodents

Rats and mice are carriers of disease but they need not be a problem on a well-managed poultry unit. The main lesson to learn is that rodents will only remain and become a problem if food and water are left lying about. All food should be stored in rodent-proof bins—an ordinary dustbin is quite adequate. Food hoppers that are suspended from the roof of the building are better than those that rest on the floor. In cases where wet mash is used it is important to clear up any food that the birds have not eaten after half an hour.

A good cat is very useful as a means of keeping rodents under control, but the cat will not earn its keep if it is called home during the day to receive a good meal. In cases where rodents become a problem, use of one of the rodent baits will normally clear it up.

Salmonellosis

This is a frequent cause of mortality among poultry and losses may occur up to ten to fourteen days of age. A post-mortem examination is necessary in order to diagnose the disease; it is also called paratyphoid, and in ducks is known as Keel disease.

The term salmonellosis is used to describe all losses due to salmonella organisms except those from *Salmonella pullorum*, and *Salmonella gallinarum*, the cause of fowl typhoid.

Birds suffering from salmonellosis and also pullorum and typhoid show few symptoms. There may be loss of appetite and diarrhoea, but frequently the first signs that anything is amiss are dead chicks. Fortunately there is a drug, known as furazolidone, available to control the disease. Survivors of an outbreak may continue to carry the disease organisms and pass on the disease to other birds. Such birds, known as carriers, should not under any circumstances be used for breeding. Rats and mice are the most frequent carriers of salmonella organisms. The bacteria remain alive for up to thirty weeks in poultry-house litter; for this reason, houses should be thoroughly cleaned and disinfected following an outbreak.

Scaley legs
Scaley leg mites are seldom troublesome in young birds but are common with older birds kept by domestic poultry keepers. The mites burrow into the skin of the legs between the scales. Irritation and swelling follow and the scales tend to break away. Suitable preparations are available and these, if properly applied, will overcome the problem. The treatment involves washing the legs of the birds with soap and water and then applying the preparation. The mites can also be eliminated by painting the affected legs with paraffin. Care should be taken to ensure that only the scaley parts of the legs are treated. Where several birds are affected it is best to treat all the birds in the pen.

Toe cutting
Breeding hens are sometimes injured during the act of mating by the sharp toes of the male birds. To avoid this type of injury to the females the last joints of toes of potential breeders may be removed. The best age to carry out this minor operation is at a day old and certainly within the first seventy-two hours of life. If toe cutting is necessary in older birds, veterinary advice should be sought.

Vaccinations
Very good vaccines are available, which are aimed to reduce losses
from Newcastle disease and from Marek's disease (pp. 83 and 82).

It is certainly advisable for laying chickens to be regularly
vaccinated against Newcastle disease. The vaccination, by whatever means, should be performed by someone who has been
properly trained for the task.

Vent gleet
This is a venereal disease of chickens and yellowish deposits may
be seen round the vent. The feathers near the vent may be soiled
and there will be often a strong and unpleasant smell. Normally,
affected birds should be killed, but in the case of exhibition birds
veterinary advice can be taken.

Worms
Many different types of worm can become troublesome with
poultry, particularly if the birds have to be kept on one patch of
land for long periods. Gape worms can cause trouble with young
chickens; the worms are small and red, about 2·5–3·8 cm (1–
$1\frac{1}{2}$ in) long and attach themselves to the windpipe. Caecal worms,
round worms and tape worms can also be troublesome. Geese
can be affected with gizzard worms, particularly if they are constantly kept on the same piece of land. The advantages of having
alternate pens for poultry can clearly be seen as part of the means
of controlling worm infections.

Slugs and earthworms can act as carriers for some types of
worm and it is thought that the earthworm can carry the parasites
for up to four years. Worms can become a problem with poultry
housed in buildings with earth floors. Individual birds may be
treated successfully. Several products are available, according to
the type of infestation. The manufacturers' recommendations
should be followed carefully.

Dressing the land round the poultry houses with copper sulphate is helpful in killing the worms. The application should be
made on a warm damp day between October and April. A mixture

of 454 g (1 lb) of copper sulphate with 227 l (50 galls) of water is sufficient for 84 sq m (100 sq yds). If worms are causing problems in houses with earth floors, the top 10 cm (4 in) may be removed, the ground treated and the earth replaced with fresh, uncontaminated soil. The copper sulphate can be applied dry, in which case 340 g (12 oz) mixed with four parts by weight with dry sand is sufficient for. 93 sq m (1,000 sq ft).

Chapter Four

Feeding and Nutrition

an egg is full of meat
Shakespeare: *Romeo and Juliet*

Principles of feeding; Nutrient requirements; Proteins; Vitamins; Minerals; Energy feeds; Palatability of feed; Daily feed requirements; Ready-made feeds; Notes on feedingstuffs (in alphabetical order); Nutrition; Make-up of the egg; Are free-range eggs best?; Value of poultry meat; Feeding systems; Feeding hoppers; Waterers; Storage of feed; Feeding young chicks; Feeding during the moult.

The easiest method of feeding, but not necessarily the most economic and certainly not the most interesting, is to allow the birds access to a constant supply of a ready-made mash bought from the local feed merchant. Although such a method of feeding is labour saving, a good deal of the fun of poultry keeping may be lost.

Relying solely on bought ready-made feeds also discounts the great advantage the small-scale producer has over the commercial farmer. The small-scale poultry keeper can reduce the feed bill by making use of feeds that do not fit into the large producers' system.

My preferred feeding programme is to buy some dry mash but also make the maximum use of feed grown in the garden and to use household scraps, stale bread when available from the baker, and some whole grain and kibbled (coarsley ground) maize.

To balance the nutrient requirements of the birds and to make the most of unusual feeds it is valuable to have at least an idea of the principles on which poultry feeding is based. One should know when and how much whole grain to give the birds, and when to increase the levels of protein. It is also valuable to have a knowledge of the individual feed ingredients to decide whether they are a good buy when they become available.

PRINCIPLES OF FEEDING

Compared with other farm animals, poultry digest feed extremely rapidly and it rarely takes more than twelve hours from the time the feed is consumed until the waste products are voided. So it is essential to ensure that the birds have a diet of high-quality feeds. They are unable to make the best use of feed that take a long time to digest, such as coarse grass and foods with a high fibre content.

A sowing programme to provide this sort of diet from home-grown feed could be: February, broad beans; March, Brussels sprouts, lettuce, lucerne, peas; April, potatoes, carrots, sun-flowers; May, beans (other than broad beans), cabbage, kale, maize; October, broad beans, cabbage.

NUTRIENT REQUIREMENTS

The nutrient requirements of most kinds of domestic poultry have been the subject of considerable research, and standards have been determined for many of the individual nutrients. In the United Kingdom the standards are those of the Agricultural Research Council, and a booklet is available from H.M. Stationery Office. The National Research Council of America also publish their own booklet and this can be obtained through booksellers.

Proteins
The body-building feeds, which are also required for egg produc-tion, are proteins. Potatoes and the cereal grains, in spite of being the main sources of energy, also supply some protein. Grains may contain from eight to twelve per cent crude protein whereas the

protein content of potatoes is only about two per cent. Cereals can, therefore, provide a proportion of the protein requirements, but not all.

Fish and meat scraps from the house are an excellent source of protein for birds as are fish meal, meat and bonemeal. These products are called the animal protein feeds. Beans, peas and soya-bean meal are also a good source of protein for poultry. The quality of these vegetable proteins is not as high as those of animal origin and they cannot form the sole source of protein for poultry. In other words, a vegetarian diet for poultry will not produce the best results unless the deficiencies are made good.

Vitamins

The requirements for the essential vitamins are minute, but their importance cannot be over-emphasized. The success of the poultry venture rests on the presence of sufficient quantities of vitamins. They are needed for good growth, the prevention of leg weakness, to help good egg production, for high hatchability and for resistance to disease.

High-quality green feed is a good source of many vitamins. Thus birds on range build up their vitamin A from eating green feed rich in vitamin A. Cod liver oil is another very useful source of vitamin A and may be used during periods when green feed is of poor quality. Birds are able to build up their own vitamin D from being exposed to the rays of the sun but in winter it is a good idea to use a vitamin D supplement. Cod liver oil is again useful for it is also a rich source of vitamin D.

The B complex of vitamins is also of considerable importance for the maintenance of poultry health. Dried brewers' yeast, dried separated milk, liver meal and fresh green feed are all good sources of many of these vitamins.

Although good quality grass, cabbage and other green crops may supply many of the essential vitamins, they are, with all vegetable feeds, deficient in one important member of the vitamin B group, namely vitamin B12. This is found only in feeds of animal origin: in fish and meat scraps, in dried and fresh separated milk and in liver meal; it is always a good idea to include some of these products in the diet for chickens. Young chicks may be provided with their B12 requirements, and many other nutritional needs at the same time, by being given separated milk to drink, either cows' or goats' milk, instead of water, and by including some chopped hard-boiled eggs in their diet.

Minerals

Poultry need minerals in their diet for bone formation, for the prevention of some forms of leg weakness and to achieve the highest hatchability. As a general rule feedstuffs of animal origin are usually well provided with minerals in a form that birds find acceptable whereas feeds of vegetable origin are generally very low in minerals.

Limestone grit or oyster shell may be used to supply calcium requirements. Calcium grit can be provided in a separate hopper. When laying at a high rate, the birds' requirements are higher than when only a few eggs are laid, but the laying bird makes a reasonable job of balancing her requirements if allowed the choice.

The total diet of the birds should contain half per cent common salt, but this does not mean this amount of salt must be added to the ration. Where much of the protein is supplied from animal sources such as fish scraps, it will generally not be necessary to include any ration of salt or any other minerals except calcium. Fish meal and fish scraps often contain a lot of salt and this must be taken into account. Salt will have to be added to the diet if the entire ration is made up of feeds of vegetable origin.

It is clear that good quality fish meal is an excellent source of protein for poultry and provides many other nutrients. These include many of the essential trace minerals, a good deal of calcium and phosphorus and many of the important vitamins, including the essential B12.

Energy feeds

Carbohydrates and fats are the energy providers and are required by poultry to maintain the body temperature of 41·7 °C (107 °F) and to meet the birds' other requirements for energy. Potatoes, maize, barley and wheat are the main sources of carbohydrate foods and these are readily digested by poultry. The diet may in fact comprise up to seventy per cent of these foods, after making allowance for the high water-content of potatoes.

Fats and some vegetable oils are excellent sources of energy for poultry but in practice one to two per cent will be the maximum that can be included in the diet without raising formidable mixing problems.

The small-scale poultry farmer must at all times ensure that the diet of his birds contains adequate levels of energy-providing feeds. Where the diet is made up of fifty to sixty per cent cereals it is safe to assume that the energy needs of the birds will be met.

They need energy to keep warm, so the feed intake will increase during periods of cold weather; this is the time the birds will appreciate those tasty, fatty bits from the dining table. In warm weather the need for energy goes down and with it the feed intake. So the percentage of the other important nutrients in the diet must be increased if good results are to be obtained. Feeding too many fatty bits at this time may mean that the birds become too fat.

PALATABILITY OF FEED

Chickens can be very pernickety about the type of feed they eat; they do not like finely-ground feeds and they dislike dusty feeds. Both are best presented in the form of wet mash if they have to be used.

Birds also dislike stale and musty feeds and much prefer fresh feed. This shows that they know what is good for them because stale and musty feeds can be the source of trouble. Like most people, birds do not like dry bread on its own and, as long as the bread is not stale and mouldy, it can be broken up and used as part of a wet mash. Any feed that swells on wetting—and biscuit meal is a good example—is best fed as a wet mash.

Palatability of feed is most important and this applies especially to ground grains. Whole grains will keep in good condition the year round if stored properly but, once ground, they soon become stale and rancid. Freshly-ground cereals only should be used and it is best to buy at weekly intervals. These rules also apply to any compounded mash used. Once feeds are mixed there may be some interaction between the various products and quality can go down. As a general rule it is best to have only sufficient ground or mixed food to last seven to ten days.

DAILY FEED REQUIREMENTS

The intake of birds depends on many things, including the temperature of the house and on the environment and, generally, the higher the temperature the less food will be eaten. The level of egg production is another great influence on daily feed consumption; although the requirement for feed to maintain the bird's body processes remains the same, nourishment needs increase as egg production rises. Maintenance requirements obviously vary according to the size of bird. Leghorns, which tend to be small bodied, eat far less feed than heavier breeds like Light Sussex or Orpingtons. Once the normal feed intake of a flock of birds has been established, any sudden drop in intake should be viewed with suspicion because this may indicate the onset of disease.

The daily intake of modern hybrid laying birds that are provided with a well-balanced ration from the feed merchant will in practice average about 110 g (4 oz) a bird. When large quantities of potatoes and household scraps are used as a wet mash, then the actual weight of feed increases considerably, because it contains about seventy per cent water, to about 170 g (6 oz).

You local agricultural feed merchant will help with details of cereals, both whole and ground, that he has available and advise on the best buy. Whole wheat or kibbled maize, or a mixture of the two, are suitable for the grain feed and bran or middlings for use with household scraps.

READY-MADE FEEDS

Feeds prepared ready made for sale by merchants are known as compounds and are generally designed to supply all known nutritional needs of the fowl concerned. Some compounded feeds are designed for mixing with ground cereals and these are often referred to as protein, vitamin and trace mineral concentrates or grain balancers.

The quality of compounded feeds generally is very high and must conform to agreed standards. The small-scale producer whose knowledge of poultry nutrition is low can buy them confident in the knowledge that they have been prepared to a very high level of quality control. Compounded feeds are available in three major forms: dry mash, pellets and crumbs, and concentrates and balancers.

Table 3: Compounds for laying chickens

Type of feed	Protein content per cent	Age for use
Chick mash or crumbs	15	0–6/8 weeks
Growers' mash or pellets	15	8–20 weeks
Layers' mash or pellets	15–17	Adults
Breeders' mash	15–17	Adults from 4 weeks before hatching eggs are required
Broiler starter crumbs	22·5	1–3/4 weeks
Broiler grower pellets	20	3/4 weeks onwards
Protein, vitamin, trace mineral concentrates and balancers	30–55	All ages

Table 3 shows the range of ready-made feeds for egg and table-meat production. Similar specialist feeds can be bought for turkeys and sometimes ducks. They are generally packed in strong paper bags containing 25 kg (about 56 lb) and are thus convenient to handle.

DRY MASH

This is feed supplied in the form of a meal and properly balanced for a particular purpose. Dry mash is usually compounded to a formula which has been computer based to help ensure the right combination of nutrients for the age and type of bird.

CRUMBS AND PELLETS

Compounded feeds are also offered in the form of small pellets or as crumbs. Crumbs and pellets are very convenient to use but usually rather more expensive than mash. Another disadvantage is that the birds may eat too many if given an ad-lib supply. The pellets should be really hard and firm and not break up easily. Soft pellets tend to break and may result in waste of feed.

CONCENTRATES

These are mixtures of minerals, vitamins and protein-rich feeds. They are designed to be mixed with the recommended levels of whole or ground cereals, and perhaps some more protein-rich feeds, to make the total diet well balanced. Often it is necessary to add further limestone or oyster shell. In other words the concentrate balances the nutrient deficiences of the vegetable-protein-rich ingredients and of the cereals.

A range of concentrates is available from local feed merchants and when buying it is a good idea to ask for full details of nutrient content of the concentrate and for any leaflets about its use. The concentrates vary in the amount that should be used; some are designed for use at a rate of ten per cent of the total diet whereas others may be designed for use at twenty or even fifty per cent rates, in the latter case the name grain balancer is often used.

Protein, vitamin, trace mineral concentrates, particularly grain balancers, are extremely useful for the small-scale poultry keeper to balance the nutrient deficiencies of household scraps and home-grown foods like potatoes.

INSOLUBLE GRIT

Flint grit and granite grit are required by poultry to allow the gizzard to function properly as a grinding machine. These grits are very hard and completely insoluble and, by helping the grinding process, enable the bird to get maximum value from its feed. Limestone grit and oyster shells are both soluble grit and cannot be used in replacement. Birds on free range are usually able to find all the grit they need but, if there is any doubt, some should be given. The amount of insoluble grit required is not large — a handful every two or three weeks for most domestic flocks of birds.

Chick-size grit should be used during the first week of life; this is then followed by medium-size grit during the growing stage, and then adult-size grit. Turkeys may be given pea-size gravel instead of adult-size grit. Cases of impaction of the gizzard are sometimes encountered and some could be due to lack of insoluble grit in the gizzard.

LIMESTONE GRIT

Good quality limestone grit can be bought in three different sizes: chick, grower and adult. The calcium in the grit is necessary for bone formation and eggshell production. Generally, laying birds can be allowed to balance their own requirements if you provide an ad-lib supply.

NOTES ON FEEDINGSTUFFS

Barley
Whole barley is not readily accepted by poultry, perhaps because the awns (beards) tickle their throats, but whatever the reason, the birds find maize and wheat far more palatable. On the other hand, once barley has been ground it becomes a very good poultry feed and may be used, as part of a mixed feed, up to forty per cent of the total diet. Barley, which has a much higher fibre content than wheat and maize, should always be finely ground to prevent the awns from becoming a problem.

Beans
Broad beans grown in the garden can be a useful protein-rich feed and may be dried and fed after cooking. The quality of the protein is such that it cannot be used to supply all the protein requirements, but beans may be used up to twenty per cent of the daily needs of adult poultry.

Biscuit meal
Biscuit meal is an excellent energy feed as part of a wet mash. The meal is very highly digestible and may be used up to a level of forty per cent of the total diet for poultry of all ages and species. Biscuit meal used with fresh or separated milk, and perhaps a little hard-boiled egg, finely chopped, is an excellent way of feeding young chicks. Meals containing chocolate residues should not be used.

Blood meal
Good quality blood meal may sometimes be available but, although it is very high in protein content, the quality of the protein is not high and some birds find the meal rather unpalatable. Up to two per cent may be used in feed mixtures for adult birds, but do not use it for young chicks. Blood meal is very rich in the amino acids lysine and methionine.

Bread

Keep on the good side of the baker, for stale bread is a useful and valuable source of food for poultry of all ages. Bread, either fresh or stale, is an excellent energy food but should be used as a part of a wet mash.

Carrots

Washed carrots are an excellent appetizer for poultry whether young or old. An adult bird may be given up to 28 g (1 oz) daily. Carrots are a reasonable source of vitamin A.

Green feed

Poultry of all ages and species find good quality green feed most palatable. In winter, when the weather makes it impossible for the birds to go out, green feed can be hung up in the poultry pen. Cabbages, kale and the last of the purple sprouting broccoli are all excellent. Once the birds are used to green feed they will eat considerable quantities and it provides them with many valuable nutrients.

Green feed contains about eighty per cent water and is, therefore a rather bulky food. It is not easy to calculate the amount of feed that can be saved by running birds on good range because of the varying types of vegetation and the quality of the green feed. In very general terms it can be estimated that an overall saving of ten per cent of the food bill may be achieved.

Young chicks do not begin to eat very much green feed until about four weeks old. The grass range for young stock should be kept in a lawn-like condition. Once the harvest has been gathered, a lot of grain is left lying in the fields and soon green feed starts to grow. Stubbles, as the fields are then called, are excellent for poultry feeding and for a few weeks birds can often find most of their own food requirements. Lucky is the person who lives beside a stubble and who can persuade the farmer to allow the field to be used for a few weeks.

Groundnut meal

Groundnut meal, also known as arachis nut, earthnut, monkey nut and peanut meal, may be used in the diet of young stock up to ten per cent of the total diet and up to twenty per cent for adults. Groundnut cannot supply the whole of the protein because it is deficient in some of the essential amino acids, notably lysine and methionine.

Poor quality groundnut meal may contain a toxin known as aflatoxin. Ducks and turkeys are particularly susceptible to its effects and may suffer heavy mortality.

Household scraps

All the scraps from the table, including fish scraps, potato peelings, bits of puddings and bacon rinds (which do not need to be chopped) are very acceptable to poultry when included as part of a wet mash. Usually the birds argue a bit about the bacon rinds, which they appear to treat as a special titbit. Household scraps, but not fish bones, are best dried off with bran or middlings, which tend to absorb some of the moisture. Use the scraps while they are fresh and do not make a habit of storing them, for this can lead to problems with vermin and of course the scraps will not stay fresh.

It is important to ensure that all scraps are cooked before being used for poultry feeding. It is, in fact, illegal to feed poultry anything which has been in contact directly or indirectly with meat or meat products of any type unless this material has been kept at boiling point for at least an hour after beginning to boil. Occasionally it may be possible to obtain waste food from a restaurant or an hotel, but such waste cannot be used without a licence from the Ministry of Agriculture.

Maize

Maize is the richest of the cereals as far as energy is concerned and often it is the best buy. Kibbled maize is eagerly devoured by chickens and whole maize by adult turkeys and it is very digestible. One of the virtues of maize is the excellent colour that it gives to egg yolks and this is particularly valuable during the winter when the quality of the grass may be poor.

The diet of laying birds may consist of up to seventy per cent maize, either kibbled or ground. Use only freshly ground maize meal. This is because maize meal soon becomes rancid and trouble can follow. Once ground, maize meal should be used immediately and by this I mean during the following week. It is important, therefore, to buy only a week's supply at a time. Whole maize, on the other hand, will keep from one year to the next if properly stored and kept out of the way of vermin. Kibbled maize keeps for longer than ground maize and up to a month's supply may be bought at a time.

Milk
Milk, in all its forms, is a first-class protein, vitamin, trace mineral food for poultry of all ages and species. The milk can be given either fresh or sour, but keep to one type; switching from fresh to sour and back again can lead to digestive troubles.

Oats
Turkeys find whole oats very acceptable, but for other classes of poultry the oats are best finely ground. Up to ten per cent oats may be included in the rations from young stock and up to thirty per cent for adults. Be on guard about oat feed. It is made up of the husks of the oats and should never be used for poultry feeding. Although this is sometimes offered for feeding, it has little value and, because of its very high fibre content, can be harmful.

Oyster shell
Oyster shell, when available, is an excellent source of calcium for eggshell production and may be used instead of limestone grit. Laying birds can be allowed an ad-lib supply.

Peas
Garden peas, fresh or cooked, are a useful source of supplementary protein. The protein is not of very high biological quality and

is rather similar to that of beans. Up to twenty per cent of the ration of laying birds may be composed of peas.

Potatoes
Potatoes are an excellent energy food for poultry of all types and particularly useful for small-scale poultry keepers who can grow their own supplies. The potatoes should be cooked, skins and all, with a pinch of salt, and then mixed with bran, middlings or biscuit meal to make up a wet mash.

Potatoes contain a large amount of water so that 100 g (nearly 4 oz) of cooked potatoes is equal in energy value to 25 g (just under 1 oz) of grain. The birds' daily ration can include up to twenty-five per cent of potatoes on a dry matter basis and this is equal to up to about 160 g ($5\frac{1}{2}$ oz) a bird daily.

Wheat
Wheat may be fed to growing and adult birds whole, but young chicks need the wheat to be cut. Up to forty per cent of the diet may be composed of wheat in one form or another. If ground wheat is to be fed it is advisable for it to be coarsely ground to prevent the flour that is formed from causing trouble. Wheat ground too finely produces a lot of flour, which can cause problems with unpalatability; the flour may stick to the inside of the beaks and cause some discomfort. Ground wheat should always be coarsely ground and then made up as part of a mixed food.

Wheat offals
Good quality milling offals, which include both bran and middlings, are particularly valuable for helping to make up a good wet mash. The offals absorb a lot of water and give the wet mash a nice crumbly consistency. Up to ten per cent milling offals may be used for young stock and up to twenty-five per cent for adults.

NUTRITION

The poultry keeper, just like the housewife, needs to know something of the essentials of nutrition so as to provide a balanced diet, whether for poultry or people, and the same basic principles apply in each case. For poultry this knowledge helps the keeper to provide a least-cost balanced diet to maintain health and production.

In nature, the egg is designed to provide the embryonic chick with all its nutritional needs during the period of incubation and also provide nutrients, in the yolk, to sustain the newly hatched chick during its first day or two of life. An egg of good quality contains a complete range of all nutrients that we also require, and which are essential for life.

MAKE-UP OF THE EGG

An egg is made up of the shell, which represents about twelve and a half per cent of the egg by weight, together with the yolk and the white, also called albumen. Eggs are one of the most digestible of the naturally occurring foods; an egg contains about twelve per cent high quality protein, about ten and a half per cent fats, a wide range of essential vitamins and, for good measure, a number of important minerals, as Tables 4 and 5 show.

Table 4: Composition of a hen's egg

	Grams	Ounces
Weight	56·7	2·00
Shell	7·05	0·25
White	35·45	1·25
Yolk	14·2	0·50

The level of vitamins and trace minerals in an egg depends upon the levels of these nutrients in the diet. Commercial egg producers invariably include a special vitamin, trace mineral supplement in layers' feed, but the supplements are designed to supply the known

requirements of the laying bird and not to obtain the highest
nutritional content in the eggs. This is illustrated by the fact that
breeding hens have higher requirements for certain nutrients than
laying hens to reach highest hatchability. Breeding birds therefore
require additional special supplements in their diet and this ex-
plains the higher cost of breeders' rations compared with layers'
feeds. The nutrient content of many commercial eggs could be
improved by a diet higher in certain nutrients.

Table 5: Dietary value of eggs—Egg Information Bureau

One egg of about 57 g (2·0 oz) supplies the following proportions
of the daily nutritional needs of a normal adult:

Nutrient	Per cent
Protein	8·00
Minerals:	
Calcium	7.00
Iron	10.00
Vitamins	
A	12.00
Thiamine	5.00
Riboflavin	18.00
Niacin*	10.00
D (approx.)	40.00
Calories	3.00

*Includes tryphophane equivalent

Size

Extra-large eggs, many of which may carry two or even three
yolks, are frequently laid by pullets when coming into production
for the first time. Usually the birds soon settle down and lay what
will become their standard-sized egg. The protein level in the diet
has an influence on egg size and a well-balanced mineral and
vitamin level is also essential to ensure the maximum number of

large eggs. An important nutrient, a fatty acid known as linoleic acid, is also linked with egg size and the best natural sources are maize and vegetable oils. The strain of the bird also has an important bearing on the numbers of large eggs laid and this is a factor which breeders may include in their selection programme.

Shell quality

Boiling eggs for breakfast can sometimes be a problem if the shells are not of first quality or if the eggs are taken straight from the fridge and into boiling or very hot water. Usually it is a minute hair crack, invisible to the naked eye, from which egg white pours. A simple gadget to prevent cracking is widely available. Before boiling, place the gadget over the broad end of the egg and press the button to pierce a small hole in the air cell of the egg.

A few poor-shelled eggs and eggs with soft shells often appear quite naturally from pullets coming into production for the first time. Generally the birds settle to normal laying within a couple of weeks. The majority of less satisfactory eggs occur at the end of the laying year and there is little than can be done about it.

Nutrition plays an important role in shell quality and thin-shelled eggs are one of the first symptoms of a diet deficient in Vitamin D. Adequate levels of Vitamin D, magnesium and phosphorus are necessary for good eggshell formation. Brittle shells have been associated with a deficiency in trace mineral manganese. An excess of magnesium may result in a loss of eggshell quality often caused by use of a poor quality Dolomitic limestone. A frequent cause of weak eggshells is a failure to increase the levels of nutrients, other than energy, during spells of very hot weather. Excess calcium may lead to the appearance of mis-shapen eggs and a deficiency of calcium can cause soft-shelled eggs.

Individual birds that persistently lay abnormal eggs should be disposed of. Another cause of a drop in eggshell quality may be bad health, such as a low-level attack of infectious bronchitis or Newcastle disease. Some cracked eggs will always be laid but the majority result from some error in management. Careful investigation should be made whenever many cracked eggs are found. Eggs should be checked for internal quality by candling (p. 54).

The shell
This consists mainly of calcium carbonate and contains many pores which allow the egg to 'breathe'. The colour of the eggshell is an inherited character (p. 21) and depends on the breed and strain, as shown in Table 11.

The white
This is also called the albumen and is made up of high quality protein of two types: thick and thin. The two thick blobs on either side of the yolk are the chalazae and they keep the yolk in position. As I have often been asked to explain, the chalazae are perfectly normal parts of the egg and do not indicate that the egg is fertile.

Occasionally the albumen may show a slight yellowish-green tinge and this means that the egg has a high nutrient content because the colour is caused by the essential vitamin riboflavin. The use of cottonseed meal in the diet may result in the appearance of eggs with albumen of a pinkish colour, which appears after the eggs have been kept in the refrigerator for some time.

The yolk
This is almost spherical in shape and is made up of not only first-class protein but also of all the other nutrients required for the developing chick. The colour of the yolk depends on the amount of pigment in the diet. Birds kept intensively on a diet without pigments can produce eggs with almost white yolks. Good quality green feed and maize are the natural sources of pigment. In the absence of green feed, yolks of reasonable colour will be obtained if the diet includes five per cent of good quality dried grass or lucerne, or thirty per cent yellow maize.

Discoloured yolks can be caused when the birds have access to unsuitable range. Heavy consumption of acorns may result in olive-coloured yolks, and discoloured yolks may appear after eating shepherd's purse, field pennycress or silage. The use of cottonseed meal may also lead to the appearance of olive-green yolks in eggs that have been cold stored. Orange-red yolks may be produced by a very small amount of pimento pepper in the diet.

The shell membrane
Immediately inside the eggshell and surrounding the white and yolk are two shell membranes which separate at the broad end of the egg to form the air cell.

Bloom
The egg is always slightly moist when laid and this film of moisture quickly dries to form the cuticle or bloom of the egg. This is a protective coat for the egg and if it is washed away micro-organisms may penetrate through the pores in the shell and infect the egg.

Pigmentation
The colour of egg yolk depends on the level of pigments in the diet. Commercial poultry keepers often include pigments in feed to give an attractive yolk colour, but the free-range hen obtains her pigments naturally by eating green feed which includes, in addition to the pigments, a large range of important vitamins and minerals. So the chances are that a free-range egg with a richly coloured yolk is nutritionally superior to one with a deeply coloured yolk laid by a hen on another system of management.

One of the advantages of running birds on good grass range or of giving them unlimited green feed to eat is that the eggs laid have really deep yellow yolks.

In some breeds of poultry, pigment is laid down in the skin and shanks; Leghorns and Rhode Island Reds, for instance, are yellow shanked whereas Light Sussex and all other varieties of Sussex are white shanked. As egg production proceeds, the birds tend to lose their pigment and the loss takes place in a definite sequence. First of all it is lost from round the eyes, followed by the beak and the shanks. The pigmentation returns in the same order when egg production ceases. The pigment is lost from the front of the shanks after 90 to 100 eggs have been laid, and from the back of the shanks after 140 to 150 eggs.

Most people in the United Kingdom prefer their table birds to be white skinned, but in some countries the preference is for deeply pigmented birds. For white meat, ingredients containing pigments should not be included in the diet for the last six weeks before the birds are to be killed. Birds kept intensively, with only limited access to green feed, are rarely heavily pigmented unless special action is taken.

ARE FREE-RANGE EGGS BEST?

Some support for the argument that free-range eggs are best comes from the 1978 Medical Research Council Report, SRS 297, from which the following figures are taken:

Table 6: Vitamin B content of eggs

	Vitamin B12 mcg per 100 g	Folic acid mg per 100 g
Free-range eggs	2·9	39
Deep-litter eggs	2·6	32
Battery eggs	1·7	25

One should not read too much into the figures, but they show that of the sample of eggs analysed the free-range eggs had fifty-eight per cent more vitamin B12 and sixty-four per cent more folic acid than the battery eggs.

Eggs are a rich source of amino acids and are one of the highest quality protein-rich foods occurring naturally. An egg of 57 g (2 oz) provides about eighty calories, which is the same as a glass of skimmed milk.

Although the shell of an egg has nothing to do with its nutrient value, a strong shell is a valuable asset for boiled eggs for breakfast. The shells of eggs laid by hens on free range are generally considered to be stronger than many laid by hens kept on other systems.

The shell is made of calcium carbonate and is sometimes eaten by people as a source of calcium. I once knew a man who insisted on two boiled eggs for breakfast every day. They had to be four-minute eggs and once he had eaten the white and the yolk he would, to everyone's astonishment, eat the shell as well. He claimed that the shells helped to keep his bones in good shape, whatever that means.

I certainly do not recommend the eating of shells as a source of calcium, but others do. I know a home economist who produces what she calls a 'peptail' which includes all the egg. The recipe runs: take four eggs and whisk, shells and all, then whisk again with a pint of chilled fruit juice and a dash of icing sugar; strain and drink. I have heard that some cooks use crushed eggshells for thickening soup.

VALUE OF POULTRY MEAT

Chicken and turkey meat is a first-class source of protein that can make a major contribution to the daily needs of people of all ages. It is well provided with many essential B-group vitamins. Because it is readily digestible it is particularly suitable for those on special diets.

Poultry meat is an extremely well-balanced source of amino acids and has a higher protein content than other meats, 85 g (3 oz) of turkey meat, for example, providing 28 g (1 oz) of protein compared with 18 g ($\frac{2}{3}$ oz) in the same amount of roast beef.

The calorie content of poultry meat is low compared with other meats. A helping of 85 g (3 oz) of chicken meat provides 162 calories compared with 327 calories from the same amount of roast beef, and 447 from 85 grams of bacon.

The meat of ducks and geese contains rather more fat than that of chickens and turkeys, so they can be kept for special occasions.

FEEDING SYSTEMS

Poultry can be managed on many different feeding systems, depending on experience and feed available. When poultry are allowed access to their feed at all times the term ad-lib feeding is used. Whatever system of feeding is adopted make sure that the birds have ample food-hopper space. Where a supply of potatoes or stale bread is available the feeding should include at least one meal daily of wet mash.

Dry mash ad-lib

The all-dry-mash system is often the most convenient in that the feed is balanced by the merchant and the hoppers only need to be filled twice weekly. Dry mash that has been properly balanced for the purpose is usually the cheapest way of buying ready-made feed. One of the objects of keeping birds on range, however, is to allow them maximum value from grass, other green feed, and insects; this will not be achieved if the birds have to spend most of their time in their houses eating dry mash, a lengthy process, so the mash must be available at all times.

Sometimes the mash becomes very dry, particularly in hot weather, and intake decreases because the birds find the feed unpalatable. When this happens, sprinkle some water on the mash to encourage the birds to begin eating again and get back to normal intake. Do not use too much water or the feed may become mouldy and caked on the bottom of the hopper.

Dry mash and grain

Another simple method of feeding is to allow the birds an ad-lib supply of a suitable grain balancer mash and to supplement this with grain. As a rule the grain balancer will be designed for use with forty to fifty per cent grain, but it is best to ask advice from your merchant. The birds may be given a small feed of grain first thing in the morning and 7–8 g ($\frac{1}{4}$ oz) a bird will be sufficient. The idea of a small morning feed, rather like an early morning cup of tea, is to give the birds a taster, but not sufficient to take the edge off their appetite and so discourage them from making the most of the grass range.

Wet mash
The wet-mash system of feeding is an excellent way of using household scraps, stale bread, potatoes and other home-produced items. I must emphasize, however, that the success of the system depends on a properly-balanced total diet.

Young chicks need to be fed on the little-and-often basis and during the first week of life require at least three feeds of wet mash daily. After this, two feeds daily will be enough, the first during the morning and the second about an hour before the birds go to roost. Allow them to eat as much as they can in half an hour and then remove all the feed that is left. Sufficient wet-mash hoppers should be provided for all the birds to eat at the same time. It is most important to clean the hoppers at least every other day and to scrub them thoroughly once a week using a disinfectant solution. If this is not done carefully, the hoppers will become sour, and rats and mice will be encouraged.

Wet mash can be made of balanced feeds alone but other feeds are generally used as part of the wet mash. The meals should contain a large proportion of feeds that are highly absorbent so it is easier to make the wet mash to the right consistency. Meals like bran, biscuit meal and middlings are excellent and so is bread. Aim to produce wet mash in a crumbly condition so that when a handful is taken up and dropped it falls in pieces rather than plopping down like a sticky, doughy mass.

Wet mash and other feeds
A more convenient way of using wet mash, rather than relying solely on wet-mash feeding, is as a means of disposing of all the household scraps and potatoes. This can be done by giving one feed of wet mash daily and supplementing it with other feeds. The best time for wet mash is as soon after the household's midday meal as possible. The morning and evening meals of the birds should be dry mash, grain or pellets or a combination of these.

A practical feeding programme is:
Early morning – kibbled or whole grain at rate of 7–8 g ($\frac{1}{4}$ oz) a bird.
Midday – wet mash made of middlings, or bran and household scraps and potatoes. As much as the birds can eat in half an hour.
Evening – full feed of balanced pellets.

Free-choice feeding

Birds can often make quite a good job of balancing their nutrient requirements themselves if they are allowed a free choice of a suitable mixture of grains in one hopper and a protein, vitamin, trace mineral concentrate in another hopper. The protein content should be about forty-eight per cent if it is to balance the deficiencies of the cereal grains. Discuss the matter with your feed merchant to make sure you buy the right concentrate. The free-choice method of feeding has also achieved reasonable success with turkeys being reared for Christmas.

Restricted feeding

The small-scale poultry keeper will not usually be concerned with feeding programmes designed to prevent overeating unless breeding, of some heavier-weight poultry for the table, is undertaken. Allowing birds, particularly meat strains, unlimited food can lead to gross overconsumption, the birds becoming far too fat for their own or the poultry keeper's good. Birds that are too fat tend to lay fewer eggs, are liable to increased mortality and, in the case of breeding birds, may lay infertile eggs. Breeders of poultry usually give advice about suitable feeding for their strains; this advice, when concerned with a restricted feeding programme, should be followed most carefully. Another aspect of restricted feeding is to delay the onset of egg production until the birds are physically mature. Again, the breeder's advice and recommendations should be sought and followed.

FEEDING HOPPERS

Always provide ample hopper space so that all the birds, the bold, the shy and the small, can feed at the same time; this is the only way to avoid bullying. The most satisfactory hopper for mash or pellets is the tubular feeder, circular in design and made of plastic. These hoppers are designed to be suspended from the roof of the poultry house and hold from 9–14 kg (20–30 lb) of food. They are held in position by a guy-rope with a hook on the end. Some tubular feeders are not suitable for mash feeding, so make sure that you buy the right design (Fig. 13).

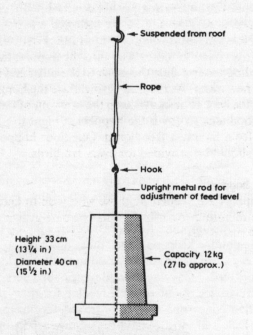

Fig. 13. Roof-suspended tubular feeder, which can be adjusted in height according to the age of the birds

Allow one tubular feeder for every twenty to twenty-five birds. The plastic tubular feeder is used extensively by commercial poultry keepers and is therefore available at an economic price. Generally it is cheaper to buy a hopper of this type than to buy the wood to make hoppers. They are suspended at such a height that the feeding lip is always kept at the height of the backs of the birds. As the birds grow, the hoppers are raised; this is an essential part of management, otherwise a good deal of feed will be wasted. Turkeys tend to bump into normal plastic hoppers and waste feed; to overcome this a special, much heavier hopper, is used.

Hoppers resting on the floor may be used and these can be of metal or wood. The hoppers should be moved to a slightly different position in the house each day to keep the litter in good condition. A special routine should be followed when filling floor hoppers. Never put new food on top of old. First, take out any litter that may have found its way into the hopper, then lift one end of the hopper and slide the mash to the other end and finally put in the new mash. As the birds grow, raise the hoppers off the floor with the help of bricks to keep the litter out of the troughs.

It is a good idea to cover the hoppers at night to prevent rats and mice from having a free board. One floor hopper 1 m (3 ft 3 in) long should be provided for every ten birds.

Wet-mash hoppers
Special hoppers are needed by those who wish to keep the food bill to the minimum by using as many home-grown foods and household scraps as possible. As a minimum, this will mean giving the birds a midday meal of wet mash. Hoppers for wet

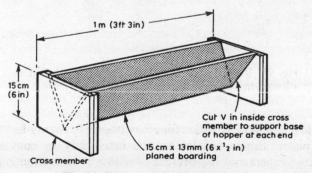

1 m (3ft 3in)

15 cm (6 in)

Cut V in inside cross member to support base of hopper at each end

15 cm x 13 mm (6 x $\frac{1}{2}$ in) planed boarding

Cross member

Fig. 14. Wet-mash feeding hopper

mash can be V-shaped and made from 1.5×15 cm ($\frac{1}{2} \times 6$ in) boards. Two pieces of planed board are nailed together at the edges with a cross member at each end (Fig. 14). One hopper of this type, 1 m (3 ft 3 in) long, will be sufficient for every ten birds. The ground round the wet-mash hoppers soon becomes worn out and so the feeder should be moved to a new position at frequent intervals.

WATERERS

Poultry of all species require a regular supply of clean drinking water and this should constantly be available during the day. Whenever possible provide the birds with an automatic supply, which is not only more convenient but ensures that the birds do not run out of water. A good supply is particularly important throughout the brooding period. Young chicks should not have to walk more than 40–50 cm (about 18 in) to the drinkers, so it is better to have a few extra drinkers for use in the early stages.

Excellent automatic drinkers are available for bantams, large chickens and turkeys. These waterers are comparatively cheap because they are sold in large numbers to commercial poultry producers. In fact it is generally cheaper to buy a new automatic drinker than to make one.

If it is not possible to arrange an automatic supply of water, the drinker should be designed so that the birds cannot foul the water with their droppings.

In winter the water may freeze and this is often accompanied by a fall in egg production. As a matter of routine all water pipes should be lagged.

Remember that during the rearing period water can be replaced by separated milk or by a mixture of half water and milk. The milk diet is particularly valuable when chicks are being reared without the help of a ready-made chick mash.

All water troughs should be cleaned daily and, at least once a week, the troughs should be washed with a suitable disinfectant.

The drinkers considered so far are all suitable for chickens, bantams and turkeys. Waterfowl, and this means ducks and geese, require a different type of waterer. It is essential for waterfowl to be able to put their entire heads in the water whenever they drink. An old washing-up bowl may be used or an old oil drum cut down. A handyman should be able, with the help of a ball-valve, to make the water supply automatic.

When water troughs are outside on the ground, the area around them soon becomes dirty unless action is taken. The trough should be moved frequently to a different spot, if possible, but, if not, the waterer should be placed on concrete slabs which must be kept clean. Clean water is always essential to birds on range and it is a good idea to prevent them from having access to stagnant water by fencing off such ponds.

STORAGE OF FEED

One of the first lessons to learn is that if food is not stored properly all the mice and rats of the neighbourhood will soon know that free feed is available and will move in. Vermin-proof bins can be a good investment; dustbins are quite good if only a small amount of feed has to be stored.

Whole wheat and maize can be stored from one season to the next and, if funds are available, almost a year's supply may be bought when the price is right. Ground cereals and meals, however, soon loose their nutritive value if stored and are best purchased every seven to ten days.

Ingredients are usually delivered in hessian sacks containing 50 kg (about 1 cwt). These are rather heavy to handle and often the bags are not in very good condition so, whenever possible, the bags should be emptied into bins and the bags returned to the food merchant for cash.

Rodent-proof bins can soon be made with a frame of wood and covered with flat galvanized sheeting. The wooden framework should be on the outside of the bins as this makes the job of keeping them clean much easier. A visit to the local scrap merchant may well prove rewarding, or old cold-water cisterns can be made into useful bins provided that the pipeholes are closed and vermin-proof lids made.

Bags of feed should never be stacked directly on the floor as this can cause feed to sweat. Wooden slatted platforms can be made using 10×5 cm (4×2 in) wood as the bearers and $5 \times 2 \cdot 5$ cm (2×1 in) battens as the cross members. If bagged feed is stacked on pallets it makes it easier to spot rats and mice and to eradicate them.

FEEDING YOUNG CHICKS

It is essential to encourage young chicks to begin eating as soon as possible and this is most important if the chicks have travelled some distance from the hatchery. Delay in providing food and water may result in dehydration, which will retard growth. Use of one of the liquid, vitamin mineral products during the first few days can give chicks a good start.

One of the best ways of feeding newly hatched chicks is to put heaps of feed on brown paper or cardboard lids, provided that the edges are not too high. The paper or lids can be slightly underneath the brooder for the first day and then gradually moved away as the birds learn to eat. Some wastage takes place, but by the end of the first week normal feed hoppers may be introduced. Some tubular feeders are designed so that the base can be detached and the pan used on its own during the first few days.

Unless careful attention is paid to day-to-day management, considerable amounts of food can be wasted on the floor. Often the wastage is not noticed because the feed soon becomes mixed with the litter and is not easily seen. Waste often results from the overfilling of feed hoppers: floor feeders should never be more than one third full and tubular feeders half full. Another frequent cause of waste is failure to raise the height of the feeders as the birds grow.

Careful adjustment of the tubular feeder is important and there is a tendency to allow too much feed to collect in the base. A depth of $1 \cdot 5$ cm ($\frac{1}{2}$ in) is ample and the temptation to tap the side of the feeder to shake more feed down into the base should be resisted.

Rats and mice can soon consume a lot of expensive feed and, as these rodents tend to come out at night to feed, the loss is not always apparent. There is far less risk of feed loss from rodents when tubular feeders are used.

FEEDING DURING THE MOULT

The annual moult, during which the birds lose their coat, means that feed requirements, particularly for protein to build new feathers, are high, but this is the wrong time to make drastic changes in their diet. A little more grain may be given once the moult is well under way, but otherwise continue with the same general formula. It is important to handle the birds regularly to ensure that they remain in good physical condition. Once the birds are coming through the moult, feed them well and allow access to limestone grit or oyster shell for the eggs they are going to produce.

Chapter Five

Ducks, Geese, Turkeys and Guinea-fowl

Four ducks on a pond,
A grass bank beyond,
A blue sky of spring,
White clouds on the wing;
What a little thing
To remember for years—
To remember with tears
                    William Allingham

Ducks: Breeds; Breeding and incubation; Sexing; Rearing and housing; Food consumption; Feeding space; Target weights; Killing and plucking;
Geese: Breeds; Housing; Egg production; Incubation; Sexing; Feeding; Killing and plucking;
Turkeys: Breeding and incubation; Varieties; Rearing and housing; Feeding; Needs of intensively-kept turkeys;
Guinea-fowl: Feeding.

DUCKS

Ducks can be kept for delicious roast duck, for the distinctive flavour of their eggs, for exhibition purposes, or for the pleasure of seeing them in a garden setting. All breeds of duck, with the exception of the Muscovy, are thought to have been developed from the wild Mallard. The Muscovy is regarded as a separate species although some people consider that these birds are not ducks but really geese.

Table 7: Domestic breeds of duck classified by the British Waterfowl Association

	Males		Females	
	Weights			
	kg	lb	kg	lb
Aylesbury	4·5	10	4·0	9
Campbell	2·2–2·4	5–5$\frac{1}{2}$	2·0–2·2	4$\frac{1}{2}$–5
Cayuga	3·6	8	3·2	7
Crested	3·2	7	2·7	6
Indian Runner	1·6–2·2	3$\frac{1}{2}$–5	1·4–2·0	3–4$\frac{1}{2}$
Muscovy	4·5–6·4	10–14	2·2–3·1	5–7
Orpington	2·2–3·3	5–7$\frac{1}{2}$	2·2–3·1	5–7
Pekin	4·0	9	3·6	8
Rouen	4·5	10	4·0	9

Table breeds

Table ducks vary considerably in liveweight and in number of hatching eggs produced. The standard weights approved by the Poultry Club are shown in Table 7, but the specially-selected table strains are very much heavier than the pure breeds. With the exception of Rouen ducks, ducks, geese, turkeys and guinea-fowl mature at about five months.

Aylesbury

The Aylesbury, with its pure white plumage, is regarded as the finest pure breed of table duck. It carries an abundance of creamy-white flesh and lays white-shelled eggs. No one really knows how the Aylesbury was developed but no doubt it was perfected over the centuries by the small-scale table-duck producers who lived in the Vale of Aylesbury, Buckinghamshire. In the annual Caldicot Duck Races, organized in aid of charity, young Aylesbury ducks generally prove more successful than the much lighter Indian Runners, which one would expect to lead the field.

Muscovy

The Muscovy, also known as the Barbary duck, originated in South America, and is a different species from all other breeds of domestic duck; this is shown when they are crossed with other ducks, for the progeny are all sterile. It makes good, gamey eating and lays white eggs.

The male Muscovy reaches nearly double the weight of the female but does not carry the curved tail feathers that characterize other breeds of duck. The Muscovy drake is also distinguished by a knob on its head. There are seven varieties of Muscovy and one of their attributes is that they graze grass very much in the same manner as geese. Muscovy ducks could at one time always be seen on the roof garden of the former Derry and Toms building in Kensington and were a great attraction. The Muscovies were no doubt chosen for this privileged role because, unlike other ducks, neither sex can quack!

Pekin

The Pekin duck, which is sleeker than the Aylesbury and also lighter in weight, originated in China and was the duck on which the American table-duck industry was developed. Pekins were introduced into the United Kingdom in the nineteenth century. The plumage of the Pekin is creamy white and the eggs have white shells. Egg production is usually superior to that of the Aylesbury.

Rouen

I always regard the Rouen as being one of the most beautiful breeds of duck and it is very similar, in plumage colour, to that of the wild Mallard. The Rouen is a well-fleshed table duck that was developed in France and has its own distinctive taste. The eggs, unlike those of the Aylesbury and Pekin, have green shells. The Rouen grows rather more slowly than the Aylesbury and matures at about six months.

Hybrid table strains

The majority of ducks now used for providing roast duck with

green peas have been developed from the pure breeds by selection
and breeding programmes designed to improve their economic
qualities. These strains are now vastly superior to the pure breeds
from which they have been developed. The credit for producing
these remarkable table ducks must go to British breeders, whose
stock is now being distributed throughout the world. The popular
hybrid strains are now regularly killed at about forty-nine days at
liveweights of 3 kg (6·6 lb).

Egg-producing breeds

The most efficient laying breeds of duck are Khaki Campbells and
Indian Runners and averages of 300 eggs a duck are frequently
achieved in the laying year. The breeding ducks of these strains
also lay at almost the same rate. Many people value duck eggs
because of their flavour but, unfortunately, the public demand
for duck eggs is small, mainly owing to the few outbreaks of
salmonella infection with which duck eggs have been associated.
The shell of the duck egg is much more porous than that of the
chicken; this means that if the shell is soiled by droppings or mud,
micro-organisms may gain entry to the egg.

Ducks are inclined to be rather messy and, unless the standard
of management is very high, many of the eggs will become badly
soiled almost immediately after being laid. Ducks tend to lay
their eggs before nine o'clock in the morning, so if they are kept in
their houses until then the bulk of the eggs can be collected immediately the birds have been allowed out on the range. Compared with the table breeds, the egg-laying breeds tend to be
somewhat nervous and flighty.

Campbell

The Campbell duck was developed in Gloucestershire by a Mrs
A. Campbell and was introduced in 1901 specifically for high egg
production. The Khaki Campbell, which was evolved from the
original Campbell, has established itself as the supreme egg layer
of domestic poultry; there have been many cases where Khaki
Campbell ducks have laid an egg a day throughout the year.

Today there are three varieties of Campbell, the Dark, the

Khaki, and the White, of which the Khaki is by far the most popular. The Dark Campbell was developed by Mr H. R. S. Humphrey specially to allow sex-linkage to take place when Dark Campbell males are mated with pure Khaki Campbell females.

Indian Runner
The Indian Runner ducks originated in Malaya and were brought by a ship's captain to Scotland. The Runners were the first of the high egg-producing breeds and there are four varieties: Fawn and White, Fawn, Black, and Chocolate. The Runners are characterized by their upright stance and, when excited or when specially trained for exhibition, can adopt an almost perpendicular carriage.

Orpington
The Orpingtons were developed by William Cook of Orpington, Kent, who was aiming to produce a breed of duck that would have good table qualities and also lay at a high rate. The ducks have a very pleasing appearance and are available in four different plumage colours: Black, Blue, Buff, and White.

Other breeds
In addition to those already mentioned there are a great many beautiful British and foreign breeds and varieties of wild duck, which are classified by the British Waterfowl Association as ornamental. Many of them can be seen at wildlife parks.

Recently the daughter of a friend of mine, who has a young family, bought half a dozen young ducklings in haste and had visions of a plentiful supply of eggs as a means of helping the family budget. I reluctantly had to say that ducks were not really suitable for domestic poultry keeping where land for ranging was limited. Ducks are messy creatures; they really need water for swimming, although this is not essential, and their eggs are very porous. In my friend's case the problem was soon solved because the ducks turned out to be drakes and were consigned to the deep freeze!

Breeding and incubation

Duck eggs take twenty-eight days to hatch, with the exception of eggs of the Muscovy, whose incubation period is from thirty-four to thirty-six days. The hatching eggs should be cleaned immediately after collection if possible. Dry cleaning is preferable but some eggs will have to be washed. Include an approved disinfectant in the washing water, which must always be kept at a higher temperature than the eggs — 27–38 °C (80–90 °F). Follow the recommendations of the manufacturer carefully and change the washing water frequently. Once the eggs are clean, allow them to dry on wire-mesh trays and, if necessary, use a hairdryer to dry the eggs quickly.

Ducks should be encouraged to lay their eggs in nest-boxes and one way to do this is to place the nest-boxes along the sides of the duck house inside. The nests should be about 30 × 35 cm (12 × 14 in) and should be well provided with litter.

The drakes should be introduced to the ducks at least four weeks before fertile eggs are required. Swimming water is not essential for mating, but it is an advantage. One drake can be mated with up to four ducks in the case of the table breeds and up to eight ducks of the lighter egg-producing breeds. The ducks of the table breeds may lay for up to forty weeks and produce 175–200 hatching eggs. The breeding ducks of the egg-producing breeds will frequently lay up to 300 eggs in a year.

The general principles of incubation outlined in Chapter 3 hold good for duck eggs. A hatchability of seventy-five to eighty per cent should be achieved. Broody hens are excellent for hatching duck eggs and the hen will normally cover ten to eleven eggs, or can be given ten to fifteen day-old ducklings to rear.

Broody ducks, of course, will do a very good job of hatching and rearing, except for ducks of the egg-laying breeds, which seldom become broody and are not regarded as being very reliable.

Sexing

Ducklings (as the birds are known until they mature at five to six months) can be sexed at a day old but the technique needs a good deal of practice and so is not used very much in small-scale production. Generally the two sexes are allowed to grow up together until it is possible to distinguish the sexes by their external appearance.

Ducks, with the exception of the Muscovy, have a characteristic quack, whereas the drakes have a more muffled quack and on being handled may give out a harsh shriek. The drakes also develop the typical curled tail, which again is not found in Muscovy ducks.

Sex-linkage (p. 59) is also possible with some breeds of duck and this allows the sex of the day-old ducklings to be determined by the colour of their down. The Brown Muscovy male mated with the Black Muscovy female results in black-downed male progeny and brown females. Muscovies will also give sex-linkage when mated with some other breeds of duck. Khaki Campbell males may be mated with Black Muscovy females to give male progeny that are black and females brown. Similarly, the Brown Muscovy male may be mated with Black Orpington females or the Buff Orpingtons with Black Orpingtons.

Rearing and housing

Ducklings require at least twice as much space during the brooding period as chickens and it is best to allow at least 0·1 sq m (1 sq ft) of floor space per duckling up to two weeks of age, after which they should be allowed outside on to good quality grass. There is always a temptation to keep too many ducks and if they are kept on true free range conditions the stocking rate should be no more than 100 ducks per 0·4 ha (1 acre). Ducklings kept intensively require at least 0·37 sq m (4 sq ft) a duckling up to eight weeks old. It is most important to ensure that the young ducklings are not exposed to floor draughts.

Fold units, moved daily (p. 00) are very suitable for rearing, and the haybox fold can be used with success. A fold of 0·9 × 2·75 m (3 × 9 ft) will accommodate up to twenty ducklings from two to eight weeks. A suitable house for a breeding pen of one drake and up to seven ducks should have a floor area of 2·79–

3·25 sq m (30–35 sq ft) a house of, for instance, 2·5 × 1·25 m (8 × 4 ft). The roof can be of the lean-to type, in which case the rear wall need be only 1 m (3 ft 3 in) high and the front 1·25 m (4 ft). Part of the front of the house should be open and covered with wire netting. The house need not be elaborate as long as the roof is waterproof; the walls can be straw between two layers of netting or made of straw bales.

Start the brooding period with a temperature under the brooder of 29–32 °C (84–90 °F) and rapidly reduce the temperature after the first three to four days, at the rate of 3 °C (5 °F) every two to three days. Artificial heat will normally be required for the first ten days only. One infra-red lamp of 250 watts will usually be suitable for a batch of up to forty ducklings. Ducklings being reared with a broody hen will not require their foster mother after they are two or three weeks old.

They grow very rapidly and, once over the brooding period, become very hardy. At three to four weeks, according to the weather, they can be housed in simple open-fronted structures in grass compounds. Allow at least 1 sq m (1¼ sq yds) each up to eight weeks. Although the houses for ducklings can be very simple it is, in many areas, essential to make absolutely certain that they are fox proof at night. Wire netting 75 cm (2 ft 6 in) high is all that is required to keep the ducklings in their pen, but this will in no way hamper the fox who is in search of a tasty meal (Fig. 7).

Feeding

The best feed is either wet mash, made up to a crumbly consistency, or crumbs or pellets. Wheat offals are of considerable help in preparing a wet mash. Ducks find dry mash rather unpalatable and so it is not recommended.

Ducklings have very much higher requirements for the vitamin niacin than chickens and one of the best ways of supplying this is to include five per cent of dried brewer's yeast in their diet. Niacin is necessary to prevent some forms of leg weakness, and for growth.

At all ages the ducks should be given as much wet mash or

crumbs as they can clear up in half an hour, and any left over
should then be removed. Three or four feeds daily may be given
during the first week of life and this can then be reduced to two
feeds daily after the brooding stage is over.

One advantage of ducks, shared also by geese, is that special
food hoppers are not really required. The food can be put on flat
boards or galvanized iron sheets. The food can be put on the
ground, but this is not advisable for it soon leads to sour patches
of land and attracts rodents; the land and the rodents then become a disease hazard.

Ducks being reared for the table require duckling starter
crumbs and at three to four weeks change to grower pellets and
begin feeding cut grain. The effect of the grain will be to reduce the
total protein content of the final diet. The ducklings will, by this
time, also gain some of their food requirements from the grass
on which they run.

Wheat, oats and maize may be used for ducks; maize is very
palatable but do not use too much for table ducklings because the
yellow pigment of the maize may be deposited in the duck and will
give the ducklings a yellowish appearance, which is not generally
required.

After eight weeks and until point of lay, adult-size grower
pellets can be used with up to fifty per cent grain if the ducks are
on good range.

It is not always possible to buy ready-mixed foods that have
been specially designed for ducks. The preferred alternative is
chick crumbs followed by grower pellets. Grain balancer pellets
designed for chickens can also be used with grains.

Breeding ducks require an above-average diet to ensure that
they receive all the special nutrients that are necessary to give
good hatchability and first-class day-old ducklings. Specially-
designed duck breeder pellets are sometimes available but, if not,
chicken breeder pellets may be used at the rate of 170–227 g
(6–8 oz) a duck daily. The pellets may be used as they are, or as
part of a wet mash that includes household scraps. The protein
content of the final diet for breeders should be sixteen to twenty
per cent. The ducks can also be given a full evening meal of grain.

The ducks will make the most efficient use of their food if they are provided with a supply of insoluble grit such as flint or granite grit of suitable size. A little chick grit may be sprinkled on the wet mash crumbs during the first few weeks and after this the ducks can be allowed access tc a hopper of adult-size grit. An alternative is to sprinkle a little grit on the food every two weeks.

It is important to provide ducks with deep enough water to immerse their heads; this applies to all water fowl.

Typical food consumption figures, liveweights and feeding space allowances are given in Table 8.

Table 8: Feed and weight of ducks

Food consumption

Age	kg	cwt
0–4 weeks	20·5	0·5
5–8 weeks	76–101	1·5–2

Feeding space for 10 ducks

Age	Length of trough	
0–4 weeks	0·3 m	1 ft
5–8 weeks	0·6	2
8 weeks onward	0·9	3

Target weight of ducklings

Age	Liveweight		Food conversion
56 days	3·2 kg	7·0 lb	3·5:1

Killing and plucking

I find that I become quite squeamish when it comes to killing ducks, which can be killed in exactly the same manner as chickens, by dislocation of their necks. In practice, as with chickens, it is usually best to find someone to give a demonstration of killing rather than to attempt the task without previous experience.

The actual age of killing will depend on the strain. Most commercial strains and breeds of duck are killed from eight to eleven weeks of age according to their feather condition. Ducks are more difficult to pluck if there are many feather stubs to be removed. The next convenient stage to kill ducks is after they have gained their adult plumage, which is from about fifteen weeks and onward.

GEESE

Geese have passed into folklore far more than other species of domesticated poultry and the reasons for this are by no means clear. As children, we soon became familiar with Old Mother Goose and we learnt that unless we took precautions the fox would soon make off with the old grey goose. In winter we sometimes suffered from goose flesh or even goose pimples and if we developed a cold we were often rubbed with goose grease behind the ears, round the nostrils and on the chest because it was considered to have magical qualities. We all know someone who has well and truly cooked his own goose and others who are so bent on self-destruction that they kill the goose that lays the golden eggs. On the other hand, some of us are so optimistic that we count all our geese as swans. In military circles we have the strange sight of soldiers marching with the goose step. Then there is the Winchester goose, whose origins are obscure, but is really a lady of easy virtue. The dying race of bespoke tailors use a smoothing iron, which is known as a tailor's goose because the handle of the iron somewhat resembles the shape of a goose's head.

Geese at one time were the mainstay of the poor farmers and smallholders of the country for the simple reason that the geese could find most of their own food by grazing on common land. When the larger farmers started to enclose the common land the smallholders became very restless for they could see one of their few sources of income was endangered. One of the songs that they sang has survived and runs:

> It is a sin in man and woman
> To steal a goose from off the common,
> But he doth sin with less excuse,
> Who steals the common from the goose.

In autumn the value of the grazing on the common deteriorated and the geese were unable to find enough food to keep in good condition. They were sent off to market, or more often carried, and the farmer had a source of cash. One of the most popular of these markets was Nottingham Goose Fair, which is still held on the last Thursday, Friday and Saturday in October. Nottingham Fair is steeped in antiquity and gained its charter as far back as 1284.

The majority of geese are eaten in autumn and winter and at one time there was a large demand for geese for the Feast of St Michael on 29 September. Geese marketed at this time of the year were generally referred to as 'green geese' or 'Michaelmas geese' and usually weighed about six to eight pounds. They were green because they had come, or should have come, from good grass range. At other times of the year the demand is now for much larger geese, particularly at Christmas.

Table 9: Breeds of goose and adult liveweights

Breed	Males		Females	
	kg	lb	kg	lb
African	9·1	20	8·2	18
Brecon Buff	8·6	19	7·3	16
Common English	7·7–9·1	17–20	6·4–7·3	14–16
Chinese	4·5–5·4	10–12	3·6–4·5	8–10
Embden	13·6–15·4	30–34	9·1–10	20–22
Pilgrim	6·4	14	5·9	13
Roman	5·4–6·4	12–14	4·5–5·4	10–12
Toulouse	12·7–13·6	28–30	9·1–10	20–22

Goose livers have throughout history always been highly regarded as a base for many an excellent table delicacy. The Greeks used to soak the livers in honey and milk to obtain an even better flavour. The French have always specialized in wonderful goose-liver pâtés but, surprisingly, the delightful pâté de foie gras did not make its appearance until the eighteenth century. A talented cook from Strasbourg was preparing a dish with goose livers and truffles and from it evolved the famous pâté.

Unfortunately, now that we live in the days of packaged and frozen foods, restaurateurs rarely put roast goose on the menu; geese take up a lot of space in the freezer and, because the meat-to-bone ratio is poor, many chefs regarded geese as expensive.

Geese are considered to be the first species of poultry to be domesticated and have been kept for meat, for their feathers for pillows, for their livers for pâté de foie gras and for their skins for making into powder puffs. Geese also have the longest life span of all domestic poultry and generally live for upward of twenty-five years.

Geese are also reputed to be fine watch dogs and they gained this reputation as long ago as 365 BC, when Rome was being besieged by the Gauls. One night, it is claimed, the Gauls had found a route into the fortress, but they lost the vital element of surprise when the Roman geese, kept in the Temple of Juno, started to cackle. The shrill notes of the geese sounded the alarm, alerted the Romans and so raised the seven-month siege. The capital was saved.

Breeds

All the modern breeds of goose, with one exception, are thought to have been developed from the wild Greylag Goose. The exception is the Chinese Goose which is considered to have been bred by the Chinese from the wild goose of China. The liveweights of domestic breeds are given in Table 9.

African

The African is one of the larger breeds, but few are kept. The feather plumage is brown or grey and particular features of the

African are a knob that surmounts the bill and a pronounced dewlap.

Brecon Buff

The Brecon Buff is a medium-size goose that evolved in Wales. The feather colour is buff and the flesh qualities good.

Chinese

The Chinese is the smallest breed and one of the most attractive. There are two varieties, the brown or grey, and the white. The egg production of the Chinese is the highest of all breeds and an average of more than sixty eggs a goose over a laying season from February to June is by no means uncommon. The flesh of the Chinese is preferred by some people, who consider that the taste is similar to that of the wild goose.

The Common English goose

Many geese kept on farms cannot be classified as being of any particular breed and are frequently described as being Embden x Toulouse. These hardy geese are also referred to as white, grey and also grey-black geese.

Embden

The Embden, which was originally introduced to England from Germany, is one of the largest breeds. The birds are very attractive with their glossy white plumage, blue eyes and orange bills, legs and feet. The Embden is a first-class table bird.

The Pilgrim

The Pilgrim goose is so called because this breed is believed to have sailed to America on the deck of the *Mayflower* with the Pilgrim Fathers. One advantage of this breed is that sexing at a day old is possible with the best strains, and with a hundred per cent accuracy. The mating of White Pilgrim males with Light Grey females results in males with yellowish down at a day old and in females with down that is grey green.

Roman

The Roman goose, sometimes referred to as the English goose, is an excellent, small goose for the table and has an abundance of white breast meat. The plumage is white.

Sebastopol

The Sebastopol, which is very rare, is pure white in plumage colour but characterized by the silk frizzled feathers on the back, body and wings. Some of these feathers may be so long that they trail on the ground.

Toulouse

Toulouse geese came to England during the middle of the fourteenth century from France where they are kept mainly for the production of livers for pâté de foie gras. The plumage of the Toulouse is predominantly grey and white.

Ornamental breeds

Wild species of geese can be kept, provided there is sufficient range, and they will often become very tame. A pair of ornamental geese provide an endless source of interest and they require very little attention because the cost of maintenance is minimal. A pond is, of course, a great help and it is essential to protect them from foxes and other predators. A small island in the centre of a pond makes an excellent home and housing is not really required. To ensure that the geese do not fly away it is advisable to have them pinioned and, although this is a simple task, it is probably wise to call in the veterinary surgeon (p. 83).

Among wild geese there are many species and some are very colourful. A visit to one of the wildlife parks will usually lead to a source for the purchase of a breeding pair. Alternatively, consult the British Waterfowl Association.

Housing

One of the advantages of geese is that expensive housing is not required. In fact, after ten weeks the geese will be quite happy to spend their nights outside. Where there is a danger from foxes, or two-legged predators, the geese should be driven into fox-proof pens at night (Fig. 7). The house should be well ventilated and clean straw provided as litter.

Geese, if properly managed, can produce a remarkable change in the grass of a small paddock. Overstocking, however, can soon lead to unsatisfactory results and possibly to outbreaks of gizzard worms.

Like other web-footed poultry, they are not suitable for keeping if space is limited and, as a general rule, it is best to allow them four times the space given to chickens. Geese need free range to find the green food which is their staple diet. Where good quality range is available, then geese offer one of the simplest and cheapest means of providing some excellent poultry meat for the table. The goslings (as they are called until maturity) can be reared on grass from three days and by the end of the fourth week, if the range is good, can find most of their own food.

One gander will be required for a set of three to five geese. Generally the ganders of the smaller breeds can be mated with more females than those of the larger breeds. Once an individual set has been gathered together they should be kept separate from other geese for a few days. After this, however, a number of sets can be run together provided there is sufficient space. In the wild state geese tend to mate for life.

Land soon becomes overstocked if too many geese are kept permanently on one area. A reasonable stocking rate is twelve to twenty-four breeding birds per hectare (five to ten geese per acre).

Egg production

This usually starts early in the year, often in February, and continues until June. The eggs are the heaviest of all the species of domestic poultry and weigh about 200 g (7 oz). Geese can be expected to lay for many years. The number of eggs laid in the season varies from thirty to fifty according to the strain. Some strains of Chinese, Roman and Toulouse may lay considerably more.

Their eggs should be collected as soon after laying as possible and any that are soiled should be dry cleaned, using wire wool. The eggs are best stored in a room kept at 7–10 °C (45–50 °F). It is a good idea to write the date of collection on the eggshell and also the breed if a number of different breeds are kept. Goose eggs are considered strong compared with hens' eggs, but can be used to make excellent omelettes.

Incubation

For the best hatching results the eggs should not be older than seven days at the time of setting. Natural methods of hatching are by far the best although quite reasonable results can be obtained from the use of small incubators, but the cost of buying an incubator is rarely justified.

The goose herself makes the best mother and may be used towards the end of the laying season. A goose will usually cover about twelve eggs and the management is almost the same as for hens. Chickens, when used for natural incubation, should be given only the number of eggs they can comfortably cover; one goose egg can be regarded as equal to four hen eggs. A Silkie, though small, is an excellent choice and will look after two eggs, usually tucking one under each wing. Chickens find goose eggs difficult to turn and so this should be done for them. In all other respects the management follows the same general principles outlined in Chapter Three.

Goose eggs take longer to incubate than chicken eggs. The smaller Chinese eggs take twenty-eight to thirty days and the larger eggs of Embden and Toulouse, thirty-three to thirty-five days. The incubation period is somewhat flexible, so do not worry if the goslings hatch a day or so earlier or later than calculated; this is quite normal.

Artificial methods of incubation may be used and, if so, the following rules should carefully be followed. In the small hot-air incubators the recommendations of the manufacturer should be followed. Normally the machine is run at a temperature of 39 °C (102·5 F). The eggs will require turning from three to five times daily until three days before the goslings are due to hatch. After the fourteenth day of incubation the eggs can be sprayed with water at 39 °C immediately following turning. Humidity is most important and the relative humidity should be maintained at fifty-five per cent. In the last week of incubation it is a good idea to wring out a small blanket in water at 39 °C and put it on the eggs for up to an hour.

Once the eggs start to hatch the incubator should be left alone, except perhaps for removing the eggshells. When the goslings are really dry they can be taken out. There is a good chance that all the goslings will not hatch at the same time so, if some are removed, keep a careful watch on the temperature to ensure that the remaining eggs are neither underheated nor overheated.

When goslings are mature it is often difficult to distinguish them from older geese. In view of this it is a good idea to mark the young geese with a numbered leg band or coloured ring, or to mark the birds by making a slight cut in the web between the toes.

Sexing

In most cases it is not very easy to tell which birds are ganders by their appearance until they are sexually mature; on occasions this may not be until the geese are six to nine months old. Goslings can be sexed by an experienced person using the vent method.

Vent sexing is not a difficult task, but for the first time it is advisable to arrange a demonstration to be given by another goose keeper. Really experienced people can sex their geese by this method from a day old. Usually, however, the vent method is used during the growing stages as the geese are nearing maturity.

Once they are mature, it is possible to decide the sex of the geese by their general appearance and behaviour. When approached, the gander will often come out from the flock as if to defend his mates, extend his neck and hiss. The voice of the gander is altogether more shrill than that of the goose. The Chinese gander has a much larger knob on its head than the goose and this can be seen from eight weeks onward.

Feeding

Goslings have enormous appetites and should be offered chick crumbs ad-lib or wet mash made from chick mash and fed on the little-and-often basis during the brooding period. Start off with four meals a day. The wet-mash system allows the maximum use of household scraps, but the use of crumbs followed by pellets is more convenient. The wet mash should be of a crumbly consistency. As the goslings grow, a little middling, coarser ground wheat or bran may be used to dilute the chick mash.

The goslings should be encouraged to eat as much green feed as possible by gradually reducing the morning feed of wet mash or by closing the hopper of crumbs or pellets. In good weather goslings can be put out to graze at three days and after ten days they should be able to find most of their food requirements from the grass range. In the event of the goslings not having access to the grass range, they should have a daily feed of some green stuff.

Grass range tends to become of poor quality during autumn, and feeding will have to be recommended. The time to start depends on individual circumstances and it is necessary to handle the geese from time to time to get an idea of their condition. Once feeding restarts, it must be continued throughout autumn and winter until the young fresh grass of spring appears. Where, during autumn, there appears to be some green feed for the geese, an evening meal of whole grain will usually be sufficient. In other cases twice-a-day feeding will be necessary. The last feed can be given an hour or so before dusk and the geese allowed to eat as much as they can in half an hour. Any food that has not been eaten after that should be removed.

Geese selected as breeding birds do not require special feeding during the winter months and are best kept in what is called 'store' condition. An evening meal of whole grain, such as wheat, is satisfactory. Special feeding will, however, be required in the early months of the year. Breeder mash of pellets should be used and the feeding should begin six weeks before eggs are required for incubation. All that is necessary are 110 grams (4 oz) of breeder pellets a bird and perhaps a little whole grain.

At all times goslings should have a plentiful supply of water to drink and, like ducks, should be able to immerse their heads completely. Water in which geese can swim is an advantage and helps to keep their feathers clean and bright, but it is by no means essential, not even during the breeding season.

Killing and plucking
Geese may be killed for the table from nine weeks onward and, at a young age, provide a most succulent and tender dish. The best way to learn the rather unpleasant task of killing a goose is to persuade another goose keeper to give a demonstration. Killing by dislocation of the neck is a very quick and humane method. Geese should be plucked immediately after killing for at this time it is much easier to remove the feathers. Plucking geese can be a tedious business and the French often iron the feathers, claiming that this makes plucking much easier.

TURKEYS

Domestic turkeys are descended from the North American wild turkeys, which at one time were found ranging over a large part of Central and North America. The Aztec Indians used to revere turkeys and made models of pure gold to use as ornaments. Once I visited the Mexico museums in the hope of finding one of them, but none appears to have survived Cortez's conquest of Mexico.

Small-scale turkey production can be a most rewarding and interesting experience. Often it is possible to rear a small number in an outhouse that would otherwise not be used, keeping capital costs to the minimum.

The disease called blackhead is still a problem with turkeys reared on grass, particularly during the first eight weeks. For this reason many prefer to rear their turkeys intensively during the first eight to ten weeks. Fortunately there is now an excellent drug available that can be included in the diet and will largely prevent the appearance of the disease.

Table turkeys, as opposed to those kept for exhibition purposes, can be divided into three main types, the large, the medium and the mini or small-bodied turkey. The large males may weigh from 11–13·6 kg (24–30 lb) liveweight or more at twenty to twenty-four weeks. Males will usually reach an average live-weight of 5·4–6·4 kg (12–14 lb) and hens 3·2–4 kg (7–9 lb) by twenty to twenty-four weeks.

The domestic poultry keeper will generally find that the mini turkey or the medium size are more suitable for rearing than the really mammoth types. Full details of the expected rate of growth and food consumption will be supplied by breeders.

Some of the commercial strains reach enormous weights. The heaviest turkey recorded is one of 36·75 kg (81 lb ¼ oz). This record for a traditional farm fresh turkey was achieved at the British Heaviest Turkey Competition in 1989 by British United Turkeys.

Breeding and incubation
The majority of turkeys kept today by commercial producers are white feathered and the reason for this is that, when plucked, the minute white stubs do not show up, whereas black or bronze stubs do. Most commercial breeders nowadays rely more and more on artificial insemination for reproduction.

Table 10: Varieties of turkey

Beltsville White	Crimson Dawn
Blue	Jersey Buff
Bourbon Red	Nebraskan
Broad Breasted Bronze	Naragansett
Standard Bronze	The Nittany
Buff	Royal Palm
Cinnamon	The Slate

A breeding trio of one male turkey, sometimes called a stag or tom, with two hens could be used to produce upward of 100 turkey poults (young birds) during the breeding season. Each variety of turkey has its own distinctive feather pattern but, unfortunately, some of these varieties are in danger of extinction due to lack of breeders. Table 10 lists the varieties of turkey that have been developed, but not all have a standard approved by the Poultry Club.

One stag turkey can be mated with ten or more females. Each hen may lay from fifty to a hundred eggs during the breeding season and some may lay far more. The turkeys come into lay at about thirty to thirty-six weeks. The eggs range in weight from 71–85 g ($2\frac{1}{2}$–3 oz) in small turkeys up to 100 g ($3\frac{1}{2}$ oz) in the large types.

Management of broody hens and small incubators for turkey eggs is similar to that for chicken eggs. The hatching eggs should be collected three times daily and dry cleaned if necessary. Eggs used for incubation should not be older than seven days. One broody chicken will cover from eight to twelve eggs whereas a broody turkey hen will cover from fifteen to twenty eggs. The eggs take twenty-eight days to hatch.

Rearing and housing
Broody chickens make an excellent job of incubating and rearing turkeys, but it will generally be more convenient to buy a small batch of day-old turkey poults and rear them artificially. The turkeys may be brooded and reared on almost identical lines to those described for chickens but turkeys require a slightly higher temperature than chickens: 35 °C (95 °F) during the first week. Another difference is that only two-thirds of the number of turkeys can be accommodated in any given area as that needed for chickens.

Many people are under the impression that turkeys are rather frail whereas once they are about ten weeks old they can be most hardy. At this age the young turkeys can, if necessary, be kept completely out of doors during the summer and early autumn, even without cover at night, subject to providing of protection against foxes (Fig. 7). Until they are used to being outside, however, it is a good idea to provide somewhere for them to go during thunderstorms. At such times the turkeys should not be left on their own; the owner should visit them and drive them under cover. After twelve weeks they should be quite accustomed to living in the open air, but they must be provided with perches for roosting at night. When cold weather arrives they should be driven into an enclosed building at night. Straw may be used to cover the floor and the turkeys should be given plenty of room.

Feeding

Household scraps and crops grown in the garden can be used for turkeys, as already described for chickens, and the wet-mash system of feeding may be employed. Turkeys are, however, very susceptible to salt poisoning and it is not a good idea to give them very highly seasoned scraps or anything known to contain much salt.

Getting turkeys off to a good start is most important and the best system of feeding is to provide the young poults with an ad-lib supply of specially prepared turkey starter crumbs for the first four weeks, followed by grower mash. In those cases where it is not possible to buy specially designed turkey feeds, chicken feeds may be used.

After twenty weeks the growth rate of the turkeys slows down and they tend to put on fat rather than lean meat. They should, therefore, be killed by twenty weeks unless very large birds are wanted specially.

As the turkeys grow their protein requirement, in terms of the percentage of the total diet, falls from twenty-eight to thirty-two for young poults to fifteen per cent at twenty weeks.

Growing turkeys find whole grains very palatable and after eight weeks will eat large amounts if given the chance. Oats are particularly popular, but wheat, barley and maize can be used. There is no limit to the amount of cereal grains that can be fed, provided that a grain balancer mash is also used.

A simple method of feeding after eight weeks is to allow the turkeys access to a protein, vitamin, trace mineral concentrate in one hopper, and to whole wheat, oats or kibbled maize in another. The term 'free choice' is usually given to this method of feeding. The grains can be mixed together or kept in separate hoppers. In practice, free choice systems of feeding appear to be only slightly less efficient than the provision of a carefully balanced ration, but are usually much cheaper.

Turkeys, like chickens, may succumb to an outbreak of the

disease coccidiosis, particularly if they are kept intensively on litter. The disease usually occurs during the first few weeks, but the inclusion of a coccidiostat in the starter crumbs will overcome the problem.

Turkeys eat considerable quantities of grass or kale if given the opportunity and up to ten per cent of their diet may be provided this way apart from wet mash.

Turkeys on range should be encouraged to forage throughout the day and this can be done by arranging for the bulk of their balancer food to be given an hour before dusk. Balancer pellets and grains are very convenient and the turkeys can soon eat what they need. The morning feed can be a small amount of grain. In the early season when the green fodder is of a high quality the amount eaten may be almost unlimited. Green feed in the spring is usually very palatable, has a high nutrient content and contains an appreciable amount of protein. Towards the end of the season the feeding value of grass tends to be low and its very high fibre content may lead to digestive troubles. At this time of year turkeys should be given extra food in the morning and perhaps a midday meal as well.

One word of warning is necessary when turkeys are kept on range. Look out for common foxgloves; if these are present in large numbers and the turkeys eat them, severe losses of birds can occur.

My wife and I have regularly reared batches of turkeys and as a result have had some rewarding and interesting experiences. Once we decided to rear a batch of turkeys in the garage and it was my job to look at the birds last thing at night and to lock them up. A number of turkeys had been stolen in the area and so, when I was woken up in the early hours of the morning by an unusual sound coming from the garage, I expected the worst. I rang the local policeman and told him that I could hear a tinkling sound that could either be someone trying to get into the garage or someone trying to get out. I thought that perhaps I had inadvertently shut the person in on my last round of the evening. The night was pitch dark and we agreed that when the policeman came round the corner he would give a signal, my wife would switch on the lights outside the garage and I would rush out from the other direction. All went well, the lights were switched on, the policeman and I converged on the building from opposite directions. The lock and chain were in perfect order; the miscreant must be inside. The door was unlocked and the intruder rushed out and got clear away. It was a large black cat!

The turkeys were all small-type white-feathered birds and they did well. We marketed them at sixteen weeks with an average weight of 5·5 kg (12 lb) and they consumed an average of nearly 16·3 kg (36 lb) of feed each.

GUINEA-FOWL

Guinea-fowl, or Gallineys as they are known in the West of England, originated from Africa where they are still found in the wild state. Guinea-fowl are classed as poultry although they are considered to be related to the pheasant family. The very nice gamey flavour of the meat distinguishes it from duck, chicken and turkey. A guinea-fowl has an abundance of white breast meat and can provide a tasty course for a family of four with some left over for a guinea-fowl sandwich later on.

Guinea-fowl prefer to perch in trees at night and they make a good deal of noise while preparing to roost. They can also be very noisy at other times and are considered to be very good watch-dogs. The shrill shrieks of the guinea-fowl are not looked upon with favour by everyone and for this reason they should be kept only if there is plenty of room.

Young guinea-fowl may be reared on the floor, but make absolutely certain that they cannot escape or they will be very difficult to catch. The litter should be really clean and dry. Cut wheat straw may be used to a depth of about 10 cm (4 in). Guinea-fowl are susceptible to the disease known as aspergillosis, so dusty and musty litter should on no account be used. It is also a good idea to place a wire-netting screen in the corners of the brooding pen to prevent crowding (Fig. 12).

The keets, as young guinea-fowl are known, should be allowed to perch from an early age and perches can be put in the house at four to five weeks. These can be made of planed wood or skinned poles of 2.5×4 cm $(1 \times 1\frac{1}{2}$ in) and 15–18 cm (6–7 in) of perch space should be allowed per bird. It is a good idea to arrange the perches on a frame with netting below. The best way to hatch and rear a small batch of guinea-fowl is with a broody hen; the guinea-fowl hen will herself rarely go broody until perhaps the end of the season. The eggs take from twenty-six to twenty-eight days to hatch.

The management of the broody hen and the general management following hatching is almost exactly the same as for chickens. The main difference is that it is best for the young keets to be confined to a grass pen, otherwise there is a real danger of losing them.

Guinea-fowl kept on range, and this is the best place for a trio kept for interest and the occasional meal, will generally lay from sixty to a hundred eggs during the six-month laying season (March to September). If all the eggs are found, about fifty to seventy-five day-old keets will be obtained from each breeding hen, but often the results are less satisfactory than this.

Feeding
Rarely is specially designed feed available for guinea-fowl, so the alternative is to use turkey or chick feed, but make sure the feed is suitable by asking the merchant. Some turkey feed may contain an additive that is essential for turkeys but unsuitable for guinea-fowl. The method of feeding is similar to that for chickens and the most suitable system is to use crumbs followed by pellets and grain.

Chapter Six

Pure Breeds, Bantams and Shows

> Hickety, pickety, my black hen,
> She lays eggs for gentlemen;
> Sometimes nine and sometimes ten,
> Hickety, pickety, my black hen.
>
> Nursery rhyme

Pure breeds; Origin and shell colour; The Fancy; Exhibition standards; Poultry clubs; Egg production; Bantams; Feeding pure breeds; Managing of breeding stock; Feeding breeding stock; Conservation of pure breeds; Poultry in schools; Clubs for young poultry keepers; Rare Breeds Survival Trust; Domestic Fowl Trust; Harper Adams; Rare Poultry Society

---

Hickety pickety was a black hen and could have been a Black Leghorn or a Black Minorca, in which case she would be described as a pure-bred bird. Pure breeds are no longer kept by commercial farmers because their egg production, or meat qualities, are by no means as good as hybrid strains.

The many breeds and strains of chicken are thought to have been developed from birds domesticated many thousands of years ago from wild stock then in the jungles of Burma, Ceylon (now Sri Lanka) and India. No one really knows when chickens arrived in England but it was certainly before the arrival of the Romans. They, however, are said to have introduced the white-fleshed type of chicken from which the Light Sussex fowls of today were eventually developed.

PURE BREEDS

These may be classified into two groups: the 'light' or Mediterranean breeds, and the 'heavy' or Asiatic breeds. The light breeds
include the Leghorns and the Minorcas – which are lighter in
body weight than the heavy breeds and therefore need much less
food. In addition, these breeds tend to be much more flighty and
of a more nervous disposition than the heavy breeds. The light
breeds rarely become broody and as a rule lay eggs with white
shells; usually they have yellow legs and, if given access to plenty
of green feed, will also have very yellow skins.

Rhode Island Reds and Marans are examples of the heavy
breeds and they tend to lay eggs with tinted or brown shells.
Some of the heavy breeds, such as the Light Sussex and the
Dorking, have white flesh. Most of the heavy breeds are prone to
become broody, although with many strains this natural function has had its incidence reduced by selective breeding.

The Silkie, with its lovely soft, fluffy and silky plumage,
its absence of hard feathers and its prominent, erect and compact
crest of feathers on its head, deserves special mention because of
its pre-eminent position as a broody hen. Silkies, either pure or
cross-bred, are usually the most persistent broody hens of any
breed. No one knows for sure where Silkies originated except that
they are of Asiatic origin and may have come from Japan.

The White Silkie is the most popular, but other coloured
varieties are available including Black, Blue and Gold. The breed
is characterized by having five toes and feathered legs. Silkie hens
are the most conscientious broodies and usually become broody
after laying up to a dozen eggs. Their eggs are a reasonable size
and are tinted or creamy white in colour. Silkies can usually be
relied upon to incubate and brood a couple of batches of eggs a
year and often they do not mind where they sit. They can be kept
for use as broodies for a number of years, and Silkies have
carried off cups at shows at up to five or six years of age.

Auto-sexing breeds are very popular and many can be seen at

poultry shows. The first auto-sexing breed to be developed was called the Legbar and can be described as an auto-sexing Brown Leghorn; the male offspring are light in down colour and the females dark. All the new auto-sexing breeds have names which end in 'bar' and which often begin with a syllable of the pure breed from which they have been developed.

Finding a breeder of pure breeds may not be easy. One way is to study the advertisements in *Fancy Fowl* and *Poultry World*. Another is to ask the secretary of the local poultry society for advice. A full list of the pure breeds of poultry is given in Table 11.

Table 11: Pure breeds — origin and shell colour

		Shell colour			
Breed	Origin	Brown	Tinted	White	Blue
Ancona	Mediterranean		*		
Andalusian	Mediterranean		*		
Araucana	Chilean				*
Aseel	Asiatic		*		
Australorp	Australian	*	*		
Barbu d'Anvers bantam	Belgian		*		
Barbu d'Uccles bantam	Belgian		*		
Barnevelder	Dutch	*			
Brabanter	Belgian		*		
Brahma	Asiatic	*	*		
Bresse	French			*	
Brockbar	British		*		
Brussbar	British	*	*		
Burmese bantam	Asiatic	*			
Cambar	British		*		
Campine	Belgian			*	
Cochin	Asiatic		*		
Creve-coeurs	French			*	
Croad Langshan	Asiatic	*			
Dorbar	British		*		
Dorking	British		*		
Faverolle	French		*		
Frizzle	Asiatic		*	*	

Table 11 — *continued*

Breed	Origin	Brown	Tinted	White	Blue
Hamburgh	European			*	
Houdan	French		*		
Indian and Jubilee Game also called Cornish	British	*	*		
Ixworth	British		*		
Japanese bantam	Japanese	*	*	*	
Jersey Giant	American	*	*		
Kraienkoipe	European		*		
La Flèche	French			*	
Lakenvelder	Dutch			*	
Legbar	British			*	
Leghorn	Mediterranean			*	
Malay	Asiatic	*	*		
Malines	Belgian	*			
Marans	French	*			
Marsh Daisy	British		*		
Minorca	Mediterranean		*		
Modern Game	British		*		
Modern Langshan	Asiatic	*			
New Hampshire Red	American	*	*		
Norfolk Grey	British	*	*		
North Holland Blue	Dutch	*			
Old Dutch bantam	Dutch		*		
Old English Game	British			*	
Old English Pheasant Fowl	British			*	
Orloff	Russian	*			
Orpington	British	*			
Onaga-Dori, Yokohama or Phoenix	Japanese		*		
Plymouth Rocks	American		*	*	
Poland or Polish	Continental			*	
Redcap	British		*	*	
Rhodebar	British	*			

Table 11 — continued

Breed	Origin	Brown	Tinted	White	Blu
			Shell colour		
Rhode Island Red	American	*			
Rosecomb bantam	British		*		
Rumpless Game bantam	British		*	*	
Scots Grey	British		*	*	
Scots Dumpy	British		*	*	
Sebright bantam	British	*			
Sicilian Buttercup	Continental			*	
Silkie	Asiatic		*	*	
Spanish	Mediterranean			*	
Sultan	Turkish			*	
Sumatra Game	Asiatic		*		
Sussex	British		*		
Shamo	Japanese		*		
Transylvanian Naked Neck	Central European		*		
Tuzo bantam	Japanese		*		
Welbar	British	*			
Welsummer	Dutch	*			
Wyandotte	American		*		

THE FANCY

Poultry keepers who breed and exhibit pure breeds of poultry are known as 'Fanciers' and the collective noun for the hobby is 'The Fancy'. It is a fascinating hobby and one that is growing in popularity throughout the country, particularly among young people. Chickens, both large and bantams (miniature versions of the pure breeds) are by far the most popular, but there are many fanciers who keep ducks, geese and turkeys.

Poultry shows are held at all times of the year, usually at weekends, and on average there are three shows a week in the United

Kingdom. In the autumn a national show at which about 2,000 birds can be seen is staged in London. One of the largest shows of bantams is staged by the Reading and District Bantam Society, usually in February, at which some 1,500 fine specimens can be seen. Many county agricultural shows have first-class poultry sections and these are well supported by poultry fanciers.

Nowadays prize poultry are sent to shows by car and train and some travel long distances; the cost of transport can be considerable compared with the last century. Lewis Wright, writing about a hundred years ago, in his classic book on poultry, said that the cost of sending a bird to London from the north of England by rail for exhibition was as little as 3d or 4d, but today's much higher costs have not diminished the interest in breeding and exhibiting poultry.

The Royal Family has always taken a keen interest in the exhibition side of poultry, and the result was that Queen Elizabeth the Queen Mother became Patron of the Poultry Club during Jubilee Year, 1977, which was also the centenary year of the Club. The development of exhibition poultry was stimulated by Queen Victoria, who in 1843 was presented with five Cochin pullets and two cockerels. The colourful Jubilee Indian Game was named in honour of her Jubilee. Royal interest was continued by Queen Alexandra who gained a first prize with a Silkie hen at Haywards Heath Show in 1906 and a reserve for a Silkie cockerel. In 1978, the Queen Mother gained awards at the International Show with a trio of Buff Orpingtons.

EXHIBITION STANDARDS

Pure breeds of poultry are judged according to a scale of points, and complete specifications have been developed for each breed by the appropriate breed club. A book giving details of the latest standards, including colour prints of many of the breeds and feather patterns, can be obtained from the Poultry Club.

One of the functions of the Club has been to standardize the judging of birds at shows. A system of practical and oral examinations has been developed so that judges can be classified according to their abilities. It is possible to become a qualified judge of one particular breed and to undergo further examination as experience is gained.

POULTRY CLUBS

The Poultry Club (p. 164) is the overall body responsible for approving the standards on which birds are judged at shows. A non-trading organization, it looks after the general interests of the large and the bantam breeds of poultry. It was founded in 1877 and has a membership of more than 2,000.

The Poultry Club publish a year book, including a comprehensive breeder directory, which can be of considerable help in obtaining stocks. Another valuable service is a regular information sheet to members giving details of forthcoming shows.

The interests of individual pure breeds are handled by a number of specialist clubs most of which are affiliated to the Poultry Club. One of their functions is arranging for club shows.

Special mention must be made of the Rare Poultry Society, which caters for the needs of all breeds for which there is not sufficient support for an individual club. This club has around 300 members who, between them, keep about 40 different breeds. Once sufficient interest is stimulated in a breed, a new club is likely to be established. Thus the Rare Poultry Society has bred specialist clubs for Andalusians, Brahmas, Redcaps and Frizzles.

The British Waterfowl Association (p. 164) caters for the specialist needs of the domestic and ornamental breeds of geese and ducks and is a very active organization. The Association publishes an informative journal containing technical as well as general interest articles. In addition, an annual show and sale is organized. A special feature of the Association is the open days arranged throughout the year when informal visits are made to members' premises. Membership of the association now tops 1,000.

EGG PRODUCTION

The pure breeds of poultry are selected and bred to conform as closely as possible with the breed standards laid down. These standards are mainly concerned with external appearance and this is the prime reason that egg production of exhibition pure breeds rarely, if ever, equals that of commercial strains. Generally, winter egg production of pure breeds is relatively poor and the main production period is during spring and summer.

Poultry fanciers accept the lower economic qualities of the pure breeds in return for the pleasure of keeping such beautiful birds and for the sheer joy of exhibiting their stock at shows around the country.

The names of pure breeds are interesting and to some extent intriguing. There are, for example, the Silver Laced Wyandottes, which have interesting connections with America because the name was taken from that of a North American tribe of Red Indians. Then we have the Scots Grey, the White Crested Black Polish and the delightful Silver Spangled Hamburgh.

Pure breeds of poultry are found in an amazing variety of feather colours and with some most interesting feather patterns. One of the most fascinating is that of the Yokohama, which is characterized by its enormous tail. The Japanese Great National Museum in Tokyo at one time had a sickle feather of 411·48 cm and another of 518·16 cm ($13\frac{1}{2}$ and 17 ft) in length, and a tail that extended to 701·04 cm (23 ft). One of the problems with such long feathers is keeping them clean, and special perches are required. The Japanese name for the long-tailed chicken is Onaga-Dori, and no one has successfully bred these in the United Kingdom.

BANTAMS

In some cases the pure breed is represented only by its miniature version; the following have no large counterpart—Belgian, Japanese, Rosecomb and Sebright.

No one really knows the origin of the word bantam, but the name was first used, according to the *Oxford Dictionary*, in 1749. There is a region of Java called Bantam and perhaps the name, and the first imports of bantams, arrived in England from there.

Bantams are very suitable for the domestic poultry keeper whose space is limited and ideal for the enthusiast in an urban area (Pl. 13). One of the smallest bantam breeds is the colourful Sebright of which the male should weigh 623 g (22 oz) and the female 510 (18 oz). The heaviest bantams are the Indian Game (or Cornish, as the Americans call them) and the Malay.

The basic rules of breeding and the laws of inheritance apply as much to pure breeds as they do to breeds and strains developed for high egg production or meat. Compared with the very few breeders who dominate world supplies of birds for commercial egg or meat production, the breeders of exhibition poultry are legion. The reason for this lies in the laws of inheritance. The breeder of pure breeds is dealing with characters, such as feather colour and feather patterns, and these comparatively simple characters are passed on from one generation to the next. These characters are said to be highly heritable. On the other hand, the commercial breeder of egg and meat strains is dealing with very complex characters which are not highly heritable and which need the help of the computer and very large numbers of birds to give the intensity of selection required.

The exhibition breeder can see the results of his breeding policy in a few months and may demonstrate his skill at the shows. The cost of becoming a breeder of pure breeds is comparatively low and well within the reach of most people.

A typical breeding pen consists of one male and two females—a breeding trio. A cockerel can, of course, be mated with far more females, but this is not usually necessary.

In order to achieve birds with a high standard of plumage, breeders often have to practise 'double mating'. One pen will be mated with the aim of producing correctly marked males and another pen to produce correctly marked females. Double mating is also practised by breeders of the blue-feathered breeds, such as Andalusians. Blue males mated with blue females will generally produce fifty per cent blue-feathered, twenty-five per cent black and twenty-five per cent white-splashed progeny, but the mating of black males with white-splashed females will normally produce all-blue offspring. There are several other mating combinations. Anyone considering such matings should study all the possibilities before embarking on a breeding programme that might otherwise end in disappointment.

FEEDING PURE BREEDS

The general principles of feeding given in Chapter Four apply equally to the feeding of exhibition poultry whether of large or bantam type, but because the birds are kept for exhibition rather than for egg or meat production it will not be necessary to provide feeds with high nutrient density. The art of feeding exhibition poultry is to bring them into perfect condition at the time of the show. Most fanciers have their own special feeding practices, which they have developed from years of experience.

Feeding is a particularly important factor if the birds are kept on the deep-litter system or totally confined. The best method of feeding is probably the use of specially balanced diets from the feed merchant. On the other hand this eliminates a good deal of the pleasure of keeping birds and is also more expensive. Feed costs can be reduced by using a large proportion of garden produce supplemented with the use of household scraps. If a balanced-diet feed is not bought it is most important to include a ready-mixed vitamin, trace mineral supplement. An alternative is to use a protein, vitamin, trace mineral supplement. Considerable quantities of whole and cut grain may be given to pure breeds, particularly during winter months when the birds are not in production.

MANAGEMENT OF BREEDING STOCK

Birds selected for breeding should be healthy and typically representative of their breed or strain. At all times the birds should be physically mature before eggs are collected for hatching, and a good age is nine months or more. Accurate records should be kept of the matings and any birds, both male and female, that do not perform well in their first year should not be retained for a second breeding season.

The males may be considered as the most important members of the breeding pen because they are responsible for fifty per cent of the inherited characters of the offspring and are mated to a number of birds. Sometimes the males are so intent on looking after their hens that they fail to eat sufficient food to maintain their body condition. To overcome this, males should be provided with special food hoppers, suspended off the floor or on the walls of the house, at a level that is too high for the females but low enough for the males to feed. The hoppers may be filled with cereals, such as wheat or cut maize, usually called kibbled maize.

Introduce the males to their mates at least seven days before hatching eggs are to be collected, to give the birds plenty of time to settle down. One young male for every ten to twelve females is usually sufficient for pullets in their first year of production; older birds may be less active and one to five may be ample, but, as indicated on page 152, a trio is the usual starting ratio, one male to two females. The cockerel should, however, be placed with the females twice a week only, to prevent overbreeding.

Sometimes males damage the females with their toes while in the act of mating. To avoid injury from this cause, the last joint of the inside toes of the males can be removed. Toe cutting (p. 85) should be carried out within the first seventy-two hours of life. After this, veterinary advice should be taken if toe cutting becomes necessary. Sometimes the hens can be damaged by over-mating and in such cases the males should be introduced to the females twice a week; this will be quite sufficient to maintain fertility where the male has to run with only two or three females. After mating, the eggs laid by the females will usually be fertile for a week.

FEEDING BREEDING STOCK

Compared with laying birds, breeding stock require much higher levels of certain nutrients, principally certain minerals and B vitamins; these additional quantities are vital or high hatchability will not be achieved. Supplementation of the diet is necessary for about a month before eggs are required for incubation unless the birds are on first-class grass range.

Unextracted dried brewers' yeast is an excellent source of most of the additional nutrients required. With small flocks, 30 grams (about 1 oz) of dried yeast should be included in the daily ration for every ten birds. In addition, breeding birds should have access to really good free range or be given unlimited supplies of fresh green feed. Cooked fish scraps are also a useful source of nutrients. In the case of bought feeds, a breeders' mash should be used.

At all times breeders require a plentiful supply of fresh water and special care is necessary during periods of very bad weather. Warm water can be supplied in conditions when cold water might freeze, even if this means replenishing the supply several times during the day.

Allowing breeding birds unlimited food, particularly the heavier breeds and those selected for meat qualities, may lead to gross overeating and to birds with too much fat. The result can be reduced egg production and a high level of infertile eggs.

To overcome the problems of overeating by breeding birds several restricted feeding programmes have been developed by breeders. Restricted feeding is not recommended for the small-scale poultry keeper until experienced in general poultry management. These programmes require regular handling of the birds, weekly say, to ensure that the birds are maintaining body condition. Overrestriction can do as much harm as overeating. When a restricted feeding programme is used the breeder's advice should be followed.

CONSERVATION OF PURE BREEDS

The small-scale poultry breeder can play an important role in eliminating the danger of extinction now facing some of the pure breeds of poultry. The danger applies not only to breeds usually considered rare but also to commercial breeds that are household names.

The strains of hybrid poultry on which the commercial poultry producers of the world depend were all based on and developed from the pure breeds of poultry originally kept by small-scale breeders. It is these very breeds, that gave the hybrid breeders such an excellent springboard from which to develop, that are now endangered. Breeders of Rhode Island Reds and Light Sussex of the commercial type are now few and far between and the Brown Leghorn has almost disappeared.

The United Kingdom has traditionally been the stock supplier of the world. At the end of the last century and the beginning of this, American breeders imported stock from the small-scale British breeders and then developed it. Later, the well-fleshed turkeys of England were imported into Canada and America and developed into the broad-breasted turkeys of today. More recently, British breeders have developed chickens, ducks and turkeys into some of the leading strains.

All these improved strains were originally based on stock supplied by small-scale breeders. Such stock contains a multitude of inherited characters, called genes, and, as the number of small breeders goes down so does the reservoir of genes on which breeders can call. At the same time, as the breeding organizations merge one with another there is also a danger that the breeds they keep to form their own genetic pool will also dwindle. There are also dangers in the great similarity that exists among some of the competitive strains of poultry and they may be too closely related.

The vital question arising from this situation is where the commercial breeders will go to find new inherited characters to meet the demands of the future. No one can really forecast just what the requirements of the nations will be for poultry stocks in another ten or twenty years. Some organizations are now engaged in conservation, but there is a wonderful opportunity for the small-scale breeder. In addition to the aesthetic value of preserving the pure breeds, the more small breeders there are, the greater will be the genetic variation on which the breeders of the world can draw; this could well have tremendous importance for future generations.

POULTRY IN SCHOOLS

Future generations are themselves making a start in this direction because schools encourage them to keep livestock. Many children encounter poultry for the first time as part of their education. The new National Curriculum requires Primary school pupils to be aware of 'Life Processes'. This involves them in a study of living creatures. Later they are required to appreciate the need for conservation and animal welfare. Poultry keeping at school provides a useful resource for unravelling the mysteries of reproduction and for stimulating a better understanding of the national environment.

Many children keep animals at home as pets, or as a hobby, and the training and experience gained by helping to manage poultry at school provide a solid foundation for animal care and welfare, and helps to develop a humane attitude to animals in general. Whenever possible, children should be encouraged to carry out the daily routine tasks of cleaning, feeding and collection of eggs.

Most Primary schools do not have the facilities to keep poultry permanently but many schools have or borrow an incubator. A local source of fertile eggs enables them to first hatch and then care for chicks. In some areas the local Agricultural College is involved in providing resources, they may even organize regular visits to schools bringing them the chickens and chicks for children to handle. Great interest can be aroused if a hen is allowed to sit until she has successfully hatched the eggs, in a wire-fronted pen on a table in full view of a class of ten year olds. Silkies are good broodies and seem to enjoy the attention and always produce a good batch of day-olds. These may later be sold to help school funds. The children find the experience most interesting and are fascinated by the way the hen turns the eggs at regular intervals.

In rural areas there are still some schools that keep miniature versions of commercial laying-units and also rear batches of table poultry. In addition to learning how to feed and manage the birds the children have the added advantage of learning how to pluck and prepare them for the table. Such experience is a great help to those who sit for GCSE examinations in Rural Studies, Agriculture and Home Economics. Some schools have farm units that include dairy cattle, pigs and sheep in addition to poultry. Kennylands school at Bishop's Stortford and Bradfield College in Berkshire maintain small flocks of pure breeding poultry, both large fowl and bantams, which earn money for their school enterprises, entries are made in shows with great success. Essex County Show has several classes specifically for schoolchildren.

Oldborough Manor School, in Maidstone, has an excellent farm unit that includes dairy cattle, pigs and sheep in addition to poultry. A small commercial deep-litter laying unit is kept, a semi-intensive laying flock of Marans, a gaggle of geese on free range and some fine Muscovy ducks, which are allowed to reproduce naturally. Entries are made in shows, with considerable success.

CLUBS FOR YOUNG POULTRY KEEPERS

In addition to helping to care for poultry at school, young enthusiasts can join junior poultry clubs and young farmers' clubs, as I did. Perhaps I was fortunate that the first club I joined was started by S. C. Sharpe, at that time Poultry Adviser to East Sussex County Council. He was a poultry enthusiast who had earlier succeeded in breeding and developing the famous Light Sussex fowl.

Members of the club were encouraged to keep poultry and I bought six Barnevelder point-of-lay pullets, and very fine birds they were. They were some of the first Barnevelders imported into England from the Barnevelder region of Holland. We had to keep records of the numbers of eggs laid and the food eaten. The eggs were all large, very hard shelled and deep brown in shell colour.

When the Young Farmers' Federation was formed, our poultry club joined it and became a young farmers' club. I remember that in Oxfordshire in the 1950s the young farmers arranged a scheme for young people, each of whom kept about twenty-four turkeys, built his own poultry house and kept full records of production costs. The scheme was so successful that some of the young farmers, and even some of their parents, became turkey producers.

Young farmers' clubs arrange a full social programme during the winter including talks on various aspects of the agricultural scene. Many club members go on, as I did, to an agricultural college for further education (see p. 164).

THE RARE BREEDS SURVIVAL TRUST

The Trust was established in 1973 and is an organization registered as a charity, that is devoted to the conservation, study, and promotion of Britain's lesser-known breeds of domestic livestock. The Trust provides a wide range of services. Breeding units and amenity centres are approved by the Trust to ensure there are good examples of the various breeds, that they are well managed and that they contribute to the conservation of the breed. Every year a show and sale of stock is arranged at the Agricultural Centre, Stoneleigh, Warwickshire. The main centre of the Trust, featuring domestic poultry, is the Domestic Fowl Trust.

The Domestic Fowl Trust

A courageous attempt to conserve many of the beautiful breeds of poultry is being conducted at the Centre for the Preservation of Rare Breeds of Domestic Poultry which is part of the Domestic Fowl Trust in Worcestershire. The trust, established in 1975, is set in the well-established grounds of Honeybourne Pastures, near Evesham (see p. 161).

The many rare breeds, the magnificent flowers and the well-kept lawns are a welcome sight at any time of the year. In the breeding season, hatching eggs and young livestock are available.

All the birds are kept under natural free-range conditions and the waterfowl look particularly impressive. Each pen is labelled with interesting details of the origin of the species. One reads, for example, that the Sebastopol Goose, with long, curling feathers on its back and wings, came from the Crimea, that the Pilgrim Goose, which is auto-sexing, gained its name because it sailed to America on the deck of the *Mayflower*, and that Sir John Sebright developed the exciting Gold and Silver Sebright bantams in 1800. Another interesting tit-bit is that Marco Polo, in the record of his epic journey to the Orient, referred to the diminutive Silkies and said that they were the only hens to have wool on their backs.

HARPER ADAMS

The National Institute of Poultry Husbandry at Harper Adams Agriculture College (p. 165) is playing its part in conservation of domestic poultry. Nucleus breeding pens have been established of a selection of breeds of poultry that are known to have been used in developing the modern hybrid strains of laying and meat poultry. The birds are housed on the deep-litter system and provide excellent information for training in genetics and demonstrating sex-linkage.

RARE POULTRY SOCIETY

Anyone with the enthusiasm to combine small-scale poultry keeping with conservation of almost extinct breeds of poultry has

the opportunity to rear exotic and interesting fowls, many of
which made important contributions to the development of poul-
try farming. New Hampshire Reds are excellent layers and La
Bresse fowls are noted for their table qualities. American Bronze
and Norfolk Black turkeys will revive some Christmas tradition
Further information from Rare Poultry Society, Alexandra
Cottage, 8 St Thomas's Road, Great Glenn, Leicestershire
LE8 0EG.

Appendix I

Job Opportunities and Training

For young people sufficiently interested in poultry to want to make a career in the subject, there is a wide range of choice. This covers the various grades of work in actual husbandry from basic agricultural work through to management; experimental and scientific work in commercial companies or at universities and agricultural colleges; in the sales force of the poultry industry including related companies; academic work in the field of research, development and education; advisory posts in Government service; animal health and market research.

Training of some kind is valuable to help progress. A craftsman is entitled to a higher basic wage and overtime rates under the Agricultural Wages Board Wages Structure Scheme. Actual details can be obtained from the Agricultural Wages Board appointed by the Government. Formal training at an agricultural college or university is even more help to advancement in the industry. Here are some brief details:

THE AGRICULTURAL TRAINING BOARD (ATB)

This Board organizes training courses through its network of sixteen local boards covering England, Wales and Scotland. The training is essentially practical and arrangements can be made for small groups to be given instruction in any aspect of poultry keeping. Residential courses in all types of poultry management are also held at various venues throughout the country. The ATB's headquarters is at Stoneleigh Park Pavilion, National

Agricultural Centre, Kenilworth, Warwickshire CV8 2UG, where it also has a Management Training Centre.

NATIONAL COUNCIL FOR VOCATIONAL QUALIFICATIONS (NCVQ)

A new framework has now been established to reform the existing system of vocational qualifications. The aim is to simplify the structure and allow open access at any age. Each level in the NCVQ framework will relate to a range of skills, knowledge and understanding and ability to apply these in employment. The lowest level relates to jobs with a modest range of competence, while the higher levels relate to jobs with ever-increasing and more complex needs. All future courses of education and training will be linked into the NCVQ framework. Details from: NCVQ, 222 Euston Road, London NW1 2BZ.

NATIONAL EXAMINATION BOARD FOR AGRICULTURE, HORTICULTURE AND ALLIED INDUSTRIES (NEBAHAI)

The NEBAHAI, through its examinations and certificates, provides a wide range of subjects, of which poultry-keeping is one. The examinations can be taken at various places, from evening classes to agricultural colleges. Details from: NEBAHAI, 46 Britannia Street, London WC1X 9RG.

BUSINESS AND TECHNICIAN EDUCATION COUNCIL (BTEC)

BTEC is a self-financing independent organization, established by the Department of Education and Science, with the aim of promoting and developing work-related programmes. BTEC approves vocational programmes run by colleges, schools and polytechnics, and awards qualifications. These include National and Higher National Diplomas. Details from: BTEC, Central House, Upper Woburn Place, London WC1H 0HH.

NATIONAL PROFICIENCY TESTS COUNCIL (NPTC)

The NPTC was established in 1971 funded from central government sources. The Council coordinates proficiency testing services and develops and regularly updates a series of proficiency tests in crafts related to Agriculture, Horticulture and Forestry. Proficiency tests in Poultry Production are available in General Maintenance, Operation of Equipment, Handling of Stock, Routine Husbandry, Hatchery Practice, Artificial Insemination of Turkeys and Sexing of Day-old Ducks. A 'Craftsman' is someone who is proficient in one or more craft categories. Details from: National Proficiency Test Council, Tenth Street, National Agricultural Centre, Stoneleigh, Kenilworth, Warwickshire CV8 2LG.

QUALIFICATIONS

Diplomas and certificates
Further education courses in poultry education in England are concentrated at the *Lincolnshire College of Agriculture and Horticulture*, Caythorpe Court, Grantham. There are three main courses; a two-year sandwich course, the BTEC National Diploma in Poultry (NDP); a one-year full-time course, the Advanced National Certificate in Poultry (ANCP); and the National Certificate in Poultry (NCP), also a one-year full-time course.

University courses
Academics whose aim is the field of education, research or development should take a university course leading to an MSc or a PhD in Poultry. An MSc course is available at the *Scottish Agricultural College*, and a PhD course at the *University of Reading* and the *University of London*, Wye College.

The *Scottish Agricultural College* offers a one-year course leading to a Certificate in Poultry Husbandry. The College, which is part of Glasgow University, also offers a three-year course leading to a Diploma in Poultry Production.

Harper Adams Agricultural College, Newport, Shropshire TF10 8NB, concentrates on poultry education beyond NDP level. Poultry may be studied within the College's Higher National Diploma (HND) and BSc degree courses in agriculture. The College has the largest poultry teaching centre in Europe and includes commercial egg production, producing 9 million eggs per year, pullet-rearing and table-poultry breeding and growing (broilers, turkeys, guinea-fowl and waterfowl.) The unit also includes a fully free-range flock of laying hens.

The Junior Poultry Husbandry Certificate
In 1986 the Poultry Club introduced the Junior Poultry Husbandry Certificate scheme for young fanciers. The scheme is available to those under the age of sixteen either through their school or Poultry Society. The aim of the scheme is to create an interest in poultry keeping through practical involvement. All those who complete the course of study satisfactorily are given a Certificate of Junior Poultry Proficiency. Details of the syllabus can be obtained from the Secretary of the Poultry Club.

Animal health careers
Students interested in veterinary work can specialize in poultry health for a career with the Ministry of Health or with large commercial poultry companies or pharmaceutical companies, some of which control poultry-breeding companies. University degrees are required for jobs in this field.

AWARD, GRANTS AND SCHOLARSHIPS

Grants and scholarships are available to practical poultry keepers and others to enable them to increase their knowledge of their subject in the United Kingdom and abroad. Many awards are on an annual basis. Details from individual organizations, among them:

British Egg Marketing Board Research and Education Trust, 12 Astley Cooper Place, Brooke, Norwich, Norfolk BR15 1JB.

Nuffield Farming Scholarship Trust (The Secretary), Agriculture House, Knightsbridge, London SW1.

The Poulters Company of the City of London, c/o Armourers' Hall, 81 Coleman Street, London, EC2R 5BJ.

United Kingdom Farming Scholarship Trust, Agriculture House, as above.

A Career Development Loan, that can cover eighty per cent of course fees and the full cost of other expenses may be available from some banks under a government scheme. The loan may be between £300 and £5,000 for a job-related course, providing it lasts at least one week or no more than one year. Repayment commences up to three months after the completion of training, and the government pays all interest during that period.

Appendix II

Testing of Laying Stock

Following the public concern regarding salmonella, the Ministry of Agriculture introduced regulations for the testing of laying flocks. Small-scale poultry keepers with flocks of laying birds from which eggs are sold for human consumption may be under a legal obligation to have their flock tested for certain pathogenic organisms.

Flocks of not less than 100 laying birds must be registered with the local Ministry of Agriculture branch in England, with the Welsh Office Agricultural Department in Wales and the Department of Agriculture in Scotland.

The testing involves submitting dead birds and samples of fresh faeces or cloacal swabs to an authorized laboratory, and subsequently sending the results to the Ministry. There is also a requirement to keep a record of the samples collected.

The Order also requires that eggs be collected and handled in a hygenic manner. The following is a summary of the requirements:

(a) Hands must be washed immediately before and after collecting and handling eggs.

(b) Eggs must be collected at least once a day.

(c) Broken, dented or cracked eggs must be kept separate from whole eggs.

(d) Eggs must be stored in a cool, dry place.

(e) Poultry must not be allowed into places where eggs are stored.

(f) All equipment and packaging used in collection and storage of eggs must be kept clean.

CODES OF WELFARE

The Codes of Welfare for poultry consist of a series of recommendations for the welfare of domestic fowls. Copies of the Codes can be obtained from the local Ministry of Agriculture branch. The aim of the Welfare Codes is to help ensure that the system of husbandry does not cause an unacceptable degree of discomfort or distress by preventing the birds from fulfilling their basic needs. Provisions meeting these needs, and others which must be considered, include: comfort and shelter; readily accessible fresh water and a diet to maintain the birds full health and vigour; freedom of movement; the company of other birds, particularly of like birds.

The Codes also include recommendations concerning fire and other emergency precautions; ventilation and temperature; lighting; mechanical equipment; stocking rates; feed and water; and general management.

EEC REGULATIONS

The Commission of the European Communities introduced marketing regulations in 1991 which affect anyone producing poultry meat for sale. Among other things, the use of the term 'Free Range' is defined and broken down into three terms: (a) Free Range; (b) Traditional Free Range; (c) Free Range-Total Freedom.

The term 'Free Range' may only be used where the stocking rate per square metre of floor space does not exceed, in the case of chickens, thirteen birds of not more than 27·5 kg liveweight and the birds must have had during at least half their lifetime continuous daytime access to open-air runs comprising an area mainly covered by vegetation of not less than 1 metre square per chicken.

The term 'Traditional Free Range' may only be used where the indoor stocking rate does not exceed, in the case of chickens, twelve of not more than 25 kg liveweight; however, in the case of mobile houses not exceeding 150 metres square and which remain open at night, the stocking rate may be increased to twenty birds of not more than 40 kg liveweight per metre square. In addition there must be continuous daytime access to open-air runs from the age of at least six weeks to at least two metres square per chicken.

The term 'Free Range-Total Freedom' must conform to the same criteria set out under 'Traditional Free Range' except that the birds must have continuous access to open-air runs of unlimited area. Regulations also have been made for capons, ducks, guinea-fowl, turkeys and geese. Details from: The European Commission, Jen Monnet House, 8 Storey's Gate, London SW1P 3AT.

USEFUL ADDRESSES

British Egg Information Service, 126–128 Cromwell Road, London SW7 4ET.

British Waterfowl Association, Gill Cottage, New Gill, Bishopdale, Nr Ley Burn, North Yorkshire.

The Domestic Fowl Trust, Honeybourne Pastures, Nr Evesham, Worcestershire WR11.

Fancy Fowl (published monthly), Andover Road, Highclere, Newbury, Berkshire RG15 9PH.

The Poultry Club, Home Farm House, Fair Cross, Stratfield Saye, Reading.

Poultry International, 18 Chapel Street, Petersfield, Hampshire GU32 3DZ.

Poultry World (published monthly), Quadrant House, Sutton, Surrey FM2 5AS

The Rare Breeds Survival Trust, Stoneleigh Park Pavilion, National Agricultural Centre, Kenilworth, Warwickshire CB8 2UG.

Rare Poultry Books, Veronica Mayhew, Trewena, Behoes Lane, Woodcote, Nr Reading RG8 0PP.

Rare Poultry Society, 8 St Thomas's Road, Great Glenn, Leicester LE8 0EG.

USA Addresses

American Egg Board, 1460 Renaissance, Park Ridge, IL
    60068–1340, USA.

United Egg Producers, 3951 Snapfinger Parkway, Suite 580,
    Decatur, GA 30035–3291, USA.

Watt Publishing Company, Mount Morris, IL 61054–1497,
    USA.

FURTHER READING

The books mentioned below are out of print but it should be
possible to borrow them from your local library.

Farming Ladder by George Henderson, Faber & Faber Ltd.

Ministry of Agriculture publications from H.M. Stationery
    Office.

Old Poultry Breeds by Fred Hams, Shire Publications.

Practical Poultry Feeding by Feltwell and Fox, Faber & Faber
    Ltd.

Index